Improvisation the Michael Chekhov Way

Improvisation the Michael Chekhov Way: Active Exploration of Acting Techniques provides readers with dozens of improvisational exercises based on the acting techniques of Michael Chekhov.

The book features key exercises that will help the actor explore improvisation and expand their imagination through the technique. Exercises that have been successfully taught for decades via the intensive trainings from the National Michael Chekhov Association are now clearly laid out in this book, along with information on how these performance-based techniques can be applied to a script and even provide life benefits. Guidance on how to use the exercises both in a group setting and as an individual is provided, as well as tools for lesson plans for up to a year of actor training. These step-by-step exercises will allow readers to expand their range of expression, discover the joy of creating unique characters, improve stage presence and presentation skills, and find new, creative ways to look at life.

Improvisation the Michael Chekhov Way is written to be used by individual actors and practitioners as well as in group settings such as acting or improvisation courses, and to benefit anyone wishing to enhance their creativity and imagination.

Wil Kilroy is the Department Head of Theatre Arts at New Mexico State University and an AEA, SAG-AFTRA actor. Kilroy is Co-Founder of the National Michael Chekhov Association, along with Lisa Dalton and the late Mala Powers, who was executrix of the Michael Chekhov Estate. Kilroy has utilized the acting techniques of Michael Chekhov for many decades world-wide as an actor, director, and teacher, and to uplift everyday life.

Improvisation the Michael Chekhov Way

Active Exploration of Acting Techniques

Wil Kilroy

NEW YORK AND LONDON

Designed cover image: Melis Derya White

First published 2024
by Routledge
605 Third Avenue, New York, NY 10158

and by Routledge
4 Park Square, Milton Park, Abingdon, Oxon, OX14 4RN

Routledge is an imprint of the Taylor & Francis Group, an informa business
© 2024 Wil Kilroy

The right of Wil Kilroy to be identified as author of this work has been asserted in accordance with sections 77 and 78 of the Copyright, Designs and Patents Act 1988.

All rights reserved. No part of this book may be reprinted or reproduced or utilised in any form or by any electronic, mechanical, or other means, now known or hereafter invented, including photocopying and recording, or in any information storage or retrieval system, without permission in writing from the publishers.

Trademark notice: Product or corporate names may be trademarks or registered trademarks, and are used only for identification and explanation without intent to infringe.

Library of Congress Cataloging-in-Publication Data
Names: Kilroy, Wil, author.
Title: Improvisation the Michael Chekhov way : active exploration of acting techniques / Wil Kilroy.
Description: New York, NY : Routledge, 2024. | Includes index.
Identifiers: LCCN 2023022231 (print) | LCCN 2023022232 (ebook) | ISBN 9781032422893 (hardback) | ISBN 9781032422886 (paperback) | ISBN 9781003362098 (ebook)
Subjects: LCSH: Improvisation (Acting) | Chekhov, Michael, 1891-1955.
Classification: LCC PN2071.I5 K55 2024 (print) | LCC PN2071.I5 (ebook) | DDC 792.02/8--dc23/eng/20230810
LC record available at https://lccn.loc.gov/2023022231
LC ebook record available at https://lccn.loc.gov/2023022232

ISBN: 978-1-032-42289-3 (hbk)
ISBN: 978-1-032-42288-6 (pbk)
ISBN: 978-1-003-36209-8 (ebk)

DOI: 10.4324/9781003362098

Typeset in Adobe Caslon
by Deanta Global Publishing Services, Chennai, India

CONTENTS

ACKNOWLEDGEMENTS AND DEDICATIONS   VII

INTRODUCTION   1

1 EXPANSION/CONTRACTION: THE PULSE OF LIFE   5

2 THE FOUR BROTHERS OF ART: EASE, BEAUTY, FORM, AND WHOLENESS/ENTIRETY   21

3 QUALITIES OF MOVEMENT: MOLDING, FLOWING, FLYING, AND RADIATING   35

4 ARCHETYPAL GESTURES   47

5 RADIATING AND RECEIVING   59

6 THE THREE SISTER SENSATIONS: BALANCING, FALLING, FLOATING   73

7 QUALITIES AND SENSATIONS   85

CONTENTS

8 MOVEABLE CENTERS … 97

9 THE IMAGINARY BODY … 109

10 COSTUME CHARACTERS … 121

11 THINKING, FEELING, AND WILLING: THE TRINITY OF THE PSYCHOLOGY … 133

12 ATMOSPHERES … 145

13 TEMPO AND RHYTHM … 161

14 FOCAL POINTS … 173

15 PSYCHOLOGICAL GESTURE … 187

INDEX … 199

ACKNOWLEDGEMENTS AND DEDICATIONS

This book is dedicated to my beloved friends, colleagues, and mentors in the work of Michael Chekhov, particularly the late Mala Powers and the very present Lisa Loving Dalton, my Co-Founders of the National Michael Chekhov Association.

Further thanks to the many that have taught and inspired me along my theatrical journey, including but not limited to: Blair Cutting, Judith Swift, Carol Fleming, Michael Grando, Peter Lobdell, Robert Perillo, Adrianne Harrop, Marilyn and John Birks, Peggy Rae Johnson, The Jenkins Clan, Hugh O'Gorman, Chickie Thomas, Lionel Walsh, Charlie Bowles, and my many wonderful students from Santa Monica College, the University of Southern Maine, the USM Theatre Academy, and New Mexico State University.

Thank you to Melis Derya White for the photographs and the talented students who were a joy in the photo session: Shawn Pirkle, Luis Alfonso Castro, Arleth Lopez, Aslan Longoria, and Omar Moreno.

Additional thanks to my esteemed colleagues from all over the country who contributed improvisations to this text, including Lisa Loving Dalton, Gail Cronauer, Paul Hurley, Susan Schuld, Nichole Hamilton, Geoffrey Arndt, Suzanne Schmidt, Christie Maturo, Anjalee Deshpande Hutchinson, Baron Kelly, and Josh Chenard.

This book is dedicated to Sergio Chavez, who provides me with daily inspiration.

Introduction

My hope is that this book will provide you with a very accessible way to experience the acting techniques of Michael Chekhov which have brought me a lifetime of joy. The point of the work with this technique is not only to develop skill, but also to find the joyful creative artist that is YOU! The study of performance can lead to a career directly in the field, or to a myriad of other occupations in which these skills have proved to be invaluable. By exploring your creativity, you expand your imagination and make the impossible possible, allowing for you to pursue anything that your heart desires. You may not know where that pursuit will take you, but as a creative artist you can enjoy the journey with the beauty and ease that the Michael Chekhov technique espouses.

    Please note that this book is a result of my work with the executor of the Michael Chekhov estate, Mala Powers, who studied with Chekhov in classes, privately, and was coached by Chekhov on her film roles. My other longtime and much appreciated associate in this work is Lisa Dalton. As a trio, we co-founded the National Michael Chekhov Association (NMCA). The versions of the exercises and improvisations in this book are the result of decades of work which the NMCA has continuously crafted. We have found wonderful success with the many actors and creative artists that we have worked with from around the world. The ideal in experiencing this material is to be led by those steeped in the craft, and there are many organizations around the world specializing in this work. For more information on the NMCA and our training intensives, point your browser to www.chekhov.net.

For the teacher, this book will provide exercises and improvisations that can fill the typical 15 weeks of a college or school semester, with a new technique each week, or for more in-depth discovery, these could extend to a full year course. For the actor there are instructions on how to pursue these techniques when working solo so that you can still reap their benefits. For the actor cast in a production there are notes on how to apply these techniques to a script, and by working with the techniques as part of your at-home play, you will become more facile as a performer and be able to fulfill a director's vision as well as offer your individual creative input. The director could incorporate these exercises in rehearsal and apply them to any production – from characterization, to pursuit of objectives, to the creation of specific atmospheres. For the reader who may not plan to pursue performance, there is information on how working with these techniques can enhance your life, allowing you to be an artist along your own unique journey, whatever that may be.

As a young actor studying in New York City many years ago, I was subject to training which was belittling – such as being yelled at with profanity by an instructor to "get off the stage". Perhaps that technique was meant to make me tough, or show that I could succeed despite the negativity, but it did not inspire me. When I came to study at the Michael Chekhov Studio in New York, I discovered a way of working that was supportive and caring and I knew then that if I ever became an educator that would be my focus. So here I am! I hope you discover the joy and fun along with enhanced skills that working with these techniques can bring and that they propel you forward to wherever you decide to go.

FIGURE 1.1 Four actors surround the fifth actor, who is on the floor. Photograph by Melis Derya White. Actors from L to R: Shawn Pirkle, Omar Moreno, Luis Alfonso Castro, Arleth Lopez, Aslan Longoria

1
EXPANSION/CONTRACTION
THE PULSE OF LIFE

> "Open *yourself completely, spreading wide your arms and hands, your legs far apart. Remain in this expanded position...Now close yourself...Imagine that you are becoming smaller and smaller, curling up, contracting...*"
>
> Michael Chekhov, To the Actor,
> Routledge, revised 2002, courtesy of the
> Michael Chekhov Estate

This chapter introduces a basic movement that can be seen within us and in all of nature and by working with these simple movements our acting can transform. These two basic movements are contraction and expansion. By experiencing this pulse which is apparent in so much of life around us, participants are introduced to the power this acting tool holds. From character creation to connecting with feelings and images, a performer has a myriad of artistic choices from this simple dynamic of contracting and expanding.

These movements provide a rudimentary basis for the physicality of Michael Chekhov's technique and a way to analyze character. The physical exercises from the Michael Chekhov technique are known as psychophysical, meaning that while they are based in physical action, they affect the psychology, thus a psycho-physical connection occurs. The work by the body influences the mind, the thoughts, and ultimately feelings. The experience of contraction and expansion can provide a means to creating character and emotion by physical means and via the imagination. The concept behind these psycho-physical exercises is that you are able, via movement and your imagination, to conjure up anything needed for a performance. This provides an alternative to using personal experience, which for some can be problematic as old memories are drawn upon which could lead to fresh trauma. This and all the following exercises are an accessible and healthy way for performers of all ages to expand their skills and expand their talent.

Improvisation 1: Contraction/Expansion

(While this work and many exercises that follow can be done solo, you'll note that having an instructor/leader is typically more effective. However, even if with a group, beginning exercises often require a focus on individual work.)

As you ponder this technique of contraction and expansion, you may note that these movements are all around us and within us. When we pick up an object, we expand our hand, and once the object is within our grasp, we contract our fingers and hand around the object. Our heart is contracting and expanding to pump blood throughout the body. Our lungs expand to take in air, and then contract to exhale. A tiny seed expands into a plant and then during winter that plant may contract back into the soil, losing all its stems and leaves, then expand in spring once again. These contractions and expansions are a basic element of life, and Michael Chekhov encourages us to examine them in relation to character and emotion.

To initially experience these elements, simply begin in what NMCA refers to as a universal stance. This is a stance where your body is in its own best alignment with shoulders above the hips, and hips above the ankles, with the feet shoulder length distance apart and the eyes looking straight ahead with the spine feeling free and elongated – from the tailbone through the neck to the top of the head. Imagining a rope at the crown of the head gently pulling upwards can help you achieve this stance. Other pedagogy may refer to this as "actor's neutral" but, are any of us truly neutral? Instead, the universal stance encourages everyone to find their own best way to stand, their personal ideal of alignment, rather than forcing something that is too specific, while still relating to a universal balanced stance, encompassing varied degrees of individuality. From here, the actor should feel they have the capacity to move in any direction and are feeling their own ideal physical alignment.

Once the universal stance is established, slowly and deliberately begin to contract. You are simply willing yourself to take up less space physically, allowing gravity to take you toward the earth, imagining that both externally and internally every part of you is slowly contracting, folding in unto itself, becoming tighter and smaller. Pay attention to what is happening, such as changes with your breath – be sure to keep breathing! – and any feelings, thoughts, or images that arise. Once you have reached your own version of a fully contracted state, take a bit of time to experience that state of being. Allow your imagination to be active so that feelings may emerge, or specific images may cross your mind. Examine how this contracted state affects the breath. While you will want to have the exhalation happen as you vocalize, to begin simply be aware of how your body is responding to being in this state. To further examine how this state affects the voice, count out loud from one to ten, or begin reciting the alphabet. Despite the contraction, be sure to employ healthy vocal technique, with an open throat, despite the rest of the body being contracted. Be aware if a specific feeling may be inferred by the way your voice escapes the contracted body. Once you've spent just a bit of time in this state, slowly begin to expand. How does that first moment feel? How has the breath changed with that initial expansion? Slowly and deliberately continue to expand, allowing yourself to take up more and more space and when you have reached what you feel is your maximum expansion, perhaps with a wide stance and arms outstretched, imagine that you can expand further, and that you can extend your energy beyond your physical body, continuing to expand. Once in this fully expanded state, once again count out loud from one to ten or recite the alphabet. Be aware of how your voice has changed from when you recited this same list while contracted. How has your breathing changed? Now – release!

Discussion/Reflection

What sensations did you experience in each of these states? Did those sensations lead to any feelings? Did your breath change? Did your voice change? How might this relate to characters and emotion? If working on this exercise with a group, did the atmosphere of the room change from the contraction to the expansion? For some, the contracted state is extremely uncomfortable and feels restricted and confined. But for someone else it may be a feeling of protection and perhaps womb-like and comforting. These are perfectly valid responses, and the hope is to receive these varying responses. It then allows the instructor to explain that there is no positive or negative charge to either point on this spectrum of expansion to contraction. Instead, the performer will work with this basic pulse to explore character, personality, and feeling according to what may be given in a specific text.

Improvisation 2

Part 1

Once again participants begin in the universal stance. Once again, begin to slowly contract but the instructor now side coaches: "Imagine that your heart is contracting and becoming more closed off to the world. As your physical body contracts, your heart, which we are imagining right now to be the center of your feelings, is also contracting and becoming smaller and smaller".

Once you have reached your maximum contraction be aware of what sensations you are experiencing and how it feels to be in this state with a closed off heart. Be aware that what's typically known as the center of feelings, the heart, has been contracted fully so that those particular feelings are no longer available – they are tight and contracted and now hidden. Be aware of how your breathing has changed. Once again count out loud or recite the alphabet and be aware of what is happening with your voice.

Part 2

Once you have experienced this fully contracted physical state with the internally closed off heart, retain the sensations with any accompanying feelings, but rise up to standing – imagining that your heart remains contracted. Return to a fully upright position and begin to move about the space, maintaining the contraction of the heart, the closed off center of feelings. Discover the way in which you are now perceiving the world via this closed off heart. Begin to recognize that you are not alone as you walk amidst the group you are working with. How do you feel about others? What sort of energy are you receiving from them as you pass by? Continue to actively walk, but now imagine you are obligated to share some sort of a greeting with each person you pass by. This might be a word, phrase, sound, or even some sort of gesture. Don't predetermine what may happen, but instead continue to stay focused, via your imagination, on the closed off heart, and improvise your greetings for everyone you encounter. Once everyone has had the opportunity to interact, the instructor can call the actors to come to a resting position, standing, back to their universal stance, but remaining concentrated on the exercise.

Part 3

Now, the instructor asks participants to slowly expand physically and at the same time allow that closed heart to now open and expand. As the body expands, the heart follows suit, becoming larger and more open, willing to be exposed to the world. We are allowing ourselves to imagine that the heart is the center of our feelings. Once you are taking up as much room as you can, once again imagine that you can go beyond that physical limitation with your energy. Imagine the same for your heart. As you experience that your heart within you is expanded as much as it can be, imagine how the energy of that heart, of your feelings, can go beyond that limit and radiate outside you. Be aware of the sensations you experience and what feelings may arise.

Part 4

Now let the outer, physical manifestation of the expansion drop back to standing, and start to walk around the space. Continue to maintain that expanded heart – open to the world around you and everyone in that world. Be aware of how you are responding to this world around you, now that your imagination is letting you travel through this world with an expanded and open heart. Once again imagine that you must greet every person you pass by. Again, this could be with a word, a phrase, or a sound or gesture. Improvise this greeting and it may be different for each person you encounter. Once everyone has had a chance to exchange greetings, the instructor will ask the participants to come back to a place in the room where they feel comfortable, and to allow that expansion to dissipate. Now participants can "shake out" the exercise. This "letting go" of any exercise is crucial so that no residue lingers and this ritual can be created by the group. Rather than shaking out you could push the images back into the earth, or gather them around yourself, and throw the images up to the sky – whatever feels best for you and allows you to come back to a centered place. Having a ritual to end an exercise allows for a healthy distance between character and technique, and the actor.

Discussion/Reflection

What happened for you with the contracted heart vs. the expanded heart? How did you view the world differently? Did character types come to mind via the exercise? Did certain feelings arise within you? How might you apply this to a script? Typical reactions will include feeling challenged to give anyone a greeting when the heart was contracted and then being much more open and often boisterous when greeting with the open heart. Have you seen others in life behaving in the ways you observed in the room? Can you imagine that certain characters or those you encounter in life may feel that their heart is contracted or expanded and that it affects their behavior and the way they view the world? When contracted or expanded while walking were there physical manifestations that still occurred – that "leaked" out? Perhaps you felt your toes tighten within your shoes while contracted or your head lift when expanded. Did the atmosphere of the room change from the contraction to the expansion? There is no right or wrong to any of these answers, but instead all the work encourages personal awareness that can then lead to effective choices when creating a character and interpreting a script.

Improvisation 3

Continuing along these same lines, now let the focus be on the brain, on the center of your thoughts. Now as you physically contract, focus on the thoughts in your head compressing and your entire brain becoming smaller and smaller. Thoughts are now one on top of another, without any clarity, and be aware of what you are experiencing as you are physically contracted. Slowly rise to standing and begin to walk in this state, eventually sharing some sort of greeting with everyone you pass by. Then return to a spot where you can once again focus individually, and now expand physically, and internally focus on your mind expanding. The thoughts in your head now feel fully open, with plenty of space and, in fact, your thoughts feel limitless. All possibilities are open to you within your own mind. Let go of the full physical expansion and now walk once again, being aware of how you are viewing the world with this fully expanded and open mind with limitless thoughts. Then exchange greetings with everyone you pass by. Once everyone has greeted each other, return to your own space in the room and shake out the exercise.

Discussion/Reflection

What was different now that the contraction was focused on the mind? What type of character might experience this compression of thought and why? How did your experience change when your thoughts were open and limitless? What sort of feelings bubbled up from these two situations? Did the atmosphere of the room change from the contraction to the expansion with a focus on the mind? How were these different from the contraction/expansion with the focus on the heart? How were they similar?

Improvisation 4

Part 1

To be sure that neither a positive or negative charge is assigned to contraction or expansion, this exercise will show what may be opposite to the previous experiences. Beginning again in the universal stance, begin to physically contract but now imagine that you are contracting with a very comical secret. There is no need to define what that secret is but just that you know you have that highly humorous secret within you and that while you are taking up less space, you remain focused on that secret. Once you have experienced a bit of time being fully contracted with your secret, continue to focus on the secret contracted within you, but bring yourself up to a standing position and begin to walk around the space. You remain holding that comical secret within you and being aware of how you are seeing the world around you and the other "characters" within that world that are passing by. Now, as before, share a greeting with everyone you walk by. Once you have interacted, return to an open spot in the room and back to your universal stance.

Part 2

Now let your imagination focus on that secret fading away and being replaced with an expansion of anger within you. Perhaps you begin to notice that anger is within your heart, or within your mind, or perhaps most prevalent in the pit of your stomach or even in the heels of your feet. Be aware of these sensations and what feelings may arise. Physically expand the body with this quality of anger within you, extending that energy of anger beyond your physical reach, allowing that energy to permeate the space around you. Once you feel that the quality of anger has been established, drop the physical manifestation of the expansion, and walk through the space – keeping the anger within you expanded. Be aware of how you are seeing the world around you and all of those within it. No need to exchange with others this round, as the energy from everyone around you in this state of anger will most likely be palpable. Should a future scene call for this kind of energy it can be tapped and used within a safe and guided rehearsal process. After a short time, be sure to fully release this anger with a shake, some sighs, and perhaps even a moment of quickly returning to the comical secret to dispel the anger. With this much energy you may decide to quickly run to dispel it and bounce in a goofy way. Whatever positive ritual you create allows for healthy boundaries between the artistic work and your life.

Discussion/Reflection

What did the contraction with the comical secret allow you to experience? Did the sensations and feelings you experienced while focused on this contraction surprise you and if so, how? If you previously associated expansion with a "positive" feeling, how did it change when you expanded internally with anger? What characters or character types came to mind with these experiences? Does it now make sense that a contraction or expansion has neither a positive nor negative charge but instead depends upon the imagery you work with each time? You may realize that in life sometimes we double over with joyous laughter – a very enjoyable contraction. We may expand with the anger you experienced in the exercise or something not as dramatic such as an expanding frustration when encountering roadblocks in life. Realizing that contractions and expansions can be experienced with a variety of images and emotions allows this tool to be infinitely flexible for you.

Improvisation 5

Participants gather in a circle with a performance space set in the center of that circle. A simple scene is set between two characters who will approach each other and say hello, ask how the other is, then let the other know they must go. The words don't need to be exact, but simply the gist of the interaction which allows for a scene to develop depending on what is given. Qualities to apply to the expansion or contraction are on slips of paper and each of the two individuals draw a paper, see what's assigned, and then turn their backs to the circle. The quality could also be quietly whispered to each character, and ideas from above such as comical secret, closed heart, or anger could be the qualities used, or any attribute that can be expanded or contracted. With their backs turned, so that they each focus on what they are working to achieve, unbeknownst to the other, they can physicalize as much as they need to put themselves into what is called for on their chosen slip of paper. The instructor now claps, and the two actors drop the physical manifestation of what they received and walk center and exchange their lines, informed by the state of contraction or expansion they had been working on. Once the scene concludes they return to their spot, letting go of the expansion or contraction.

Discussion/Reflection

Ask the observers what they witnessed from the exchange. What kind of energy did each character exude? What do you think their subtext was? Was there a shift as the interaction continued? What would you say their relationship was? Friends? Enemies? Strangers? Did there seem to be an objective from each character? Was the "how" which is the quality, apparent in the interaction? What would you name it?

Additional samples to use for this exercise: Contract with fear, contract with laughter, contract with timidity, contract with arrogance, contract with anger, contract with delight, expand with joy, expand with sadness, expand with curiosity, expand with disgust, expand with knowledge. You may also want to apply the exact same qualities with expansion or contraction to view what happens to that same quality when it's expressed in a different way such as contracting with joy and then expanding with joy.

Improvisation 6: The expand-er/contract-er conventions (contributed by Gail Cronauer, Professional Actor, and Certified Teacher via NMCA, Dallas area)

One of the master teachers with whom I've worked attributed these thoughts to Michael Chekhov: "If you have only one tool, let it be expansion/contraction. That is the only one you need".

I love simplicity, as do many of my students. Too often there are so many concerns or questions being asked that actors are overwhelmed, incapable of action. When that happens, or when working with actors not familiar with the techniques – as in a workshop or coaching situation – I've found expansion/contraction to be very useful, yielding immediate discoveries and possibilities – and a lot of fun!

This improvisation is an activity that can involve an entire class/group; allow all to explore a simple, easily understood tool and gain proficiency using it; encourage participants to discover how complete commitment to a tool can inspire the creation of all aspects of a character: physicality, actions, thoughts, words, world view, emotional life, relationships and more; and aid participants in making connections between the Michael Chekhov work and other pedagogies or principles, such as the importance of opposites set forth by Michael Shurtleff in his book *Audition*.

NOTE: A space allowing for movement is preferable, but this could be done in a classroom with desks and limited space.

The set up

The group is divided into two more or less equal teams: the *expand-ers* and the *contract-ers*. The teams retire to opposite sides of the space.

Each team is attending a convention celebrating and promoting their eponymous philosophy and approach to life. The Expand-ers Convention is in one "conference room"/end of the space; the Contract-ers Convention, in the other.

Team members are encouraged to begin by physically and vocally exploring the tool – alone and as part of the group – to allow the many aspects of an *expanded* or *contracted* character to emerge.

An expand-er may: promote taking up as much space as possible; drive a big car; have a large family; wear/sell big clothes and shoes; sing out loud everywhere they go; "super-size" all they can; believe in a global economy; embrace all religions and ethnicities; live large and all that that implies.

A contract-er may: promote tiny houses and take very small steps, leaving a small footprint on the planet; drive small or electric cars – or none at all; decide never to have children in order to control the population; take a vow of silence or never speak above a whisper; recycle and reuse all they can; believe in home-grown and local produce; embrace a single, true religion or creed; live in the most economical way possible.

It's important to note and remind actors that neither expansion nor contraction has only positive or negative connotations. That can be a very interesting post-improv discussion!

How it begins

Initially, the members of each team are attending the convention to share and promote their unique approach to life to one another. The "scene" becomes a trade show, a series of mini TED Talks or one-on-one interactions where conventioneers show-and-tell and learn.

And then...

At some point (5 or more minutes, depending on how things are developing), it is break time.

Each team enters the space between (the "break room") and, upon encountering the other team, begins to work to convert, engage, entice, enlist, absorb their opposites. Expand-ers work to bring contract-ers to their ways of thinking/feeling/doing. Contract-ers work to "convert" expand-ers.

Be prepared for chaos! Sometimes the encounters are one-on-one. Sometimes small groups arise and "surround" a potential convert.

NOTE: Remind team members that they have an objective in terms of the other team! Contract-ers, especially, often want to run and hide in a corner. It is much more interesting for actors to explore that different tactics can be employed to achieve an objective. Other side-coaching may encourage ease or commitment to their particular tool.

Discussion/Reflection

At some point (this can be quite demanding) break is over and teams return to their original spaces to debrief with their teammates. Still in character (expand-er or contract-er), they share their discoveries with one another.

NOTE: It is very interesting and informative for the teams to remain in character and share their discoveries and challenges with the instructor and other team!

Was it possible to stay "in character": i.e., were you able to only expand or only contract or did you find yourself moving between the two opposites? Were you able to "convert" members of the opposite team – or did they "convert" you?

Part two

After a brief break (perhaps for water!), the teams return to their spaces – and switch! Expand-ers become contract-ers and contract-ers become expand-ers. The scenario is repeated!

Further discussion (post-improv)

What discoveries did you make about yourself? about others? the technique? the tool? acting? something else? Which was easier or more familiar to you: expanding or contracting? What information does that give you about your work as an actor or perhaps your choices in life? How might you use what you discovered in/learned from this experience in your acting work?

Wrap up

Work with all the various forms of contractions and expansions as given above, and find your own, so that you become facile with this technique. Fully contract and expand physically to experience the basic movement. Contract again with a closed heart and interact with the group. Expand with an open heart and interact again. Discover the differences. Contract with a closed off mind, then expand with an open mind, interacting within each state. Contract with a comical secret, interacting with others, then expand with anger (for a short time), and compare these two states. Play with various qualities applied to expansion and contraction via a simple meeting of two characters, altering the quality applied each time.

Solo application

You'll note that some of the above exercises can be done as "homeplay". Rather than homework, look forward to your chance to play with these tools of expansion/contraction on your own. While you won't have an instructor to coach you, you can still work with expansion/contraction, applying various qualities and expanding your personal repertoire of expression. This solo work will allow you to be able to respond to any adjustment a director might give you, as you "expand" your ability to fluctuate between contraction and expansion with varying imagery. You could make slips of paper for yourself akin to the list above and fully embody whatever you pull. Practice applying these to a bit of text, resulting in very different readings depending on what is chosen. This will also prevent you from falling into cliché readings, as you will have a myriad of interpretations and may even surprise yourself!

Script application

While reviewing a script, determine what level of contraction or expansion your character is in at any one moment. Often a character has a journey, such as Cinderella being contracted as she is belittled by her stepmother and stepsisters, to expanding with joy as she dances with the prince at the ball, to contracting once again when midnight strikes. The states of contraction/expansion can be noted on a number scale, with fully contracted at a zero and fully expanded at a ten. This way you can add numbers to the margin of your script to track where your character may be. This is particularly useful in film when you shoot out of sequence, to remind yourself of your character's state. Of course expansion and contraction won't be the only notes in your script, but it's an excellent starting point to understand your character's state of mind and how they approach actions.

Life application

Being aware of your own personal state of contraction or expansion can allow you to alter that state should you wish. Perhaps you are feeling contracted and closed off from others, but know you want to be a good listener when a friend requests a visit. While it may seem a bit "goofy", take a moment to physically expand and imagine you can open your heart to be receptive to your friend, as it can make a difference. Perhaps you may want to expand when you know you need to publicly present an idea or a request. Perhaps you are feeling too expanded and "all over the place" and you need to find more calmness by contracting. Physically contracting with a quality of peacefulness and imagining a lightness in the mind, can bring you to a calmer state. You may want to contract when you realize you are hogging the limelight to be sure others are fully heard. Being more aware of these states of contraction and expansion in life will allow you to select how to pursue your goals in a more fruitful way. Being aware of these qualities will also allow you more empathy toward others, understanding their level of comfort with expansion or contraction, and what might be going on under the surface.

FIGURE 2.1 Five actors at varied levels posing with chairs. Photograph by Melis Derya White. Actors from L to R: Omar Moreno, Luis Alfonso Castro, Arleth Lopez, Aslan Longoria, Shawn Pirkle

2

THE FOUR BROTHERS OF ART

EASE, BEAUTY, FORM, AND WHOLENESS/ENTIRETY

"Ease relaxes your body and spirit; therefore it is also much akin to humor...An even better illustration is a fine clown who falls 'heavily' to the ground, but with such artistic grace and ease that you cannot restrain your laughter".

"To create with clear-cut forms is an ability which artists in all crafts can and perforce must develop to a high degree".

"Ugliness expressed on the stage by unaesthetic means irritates the nerves of the audience. The effect of such a performance is physiological rather than psychological. The uplifting influence of art remains paralyzed in such cases. But aesthetically performed, an unpleasant theme, character or situation preserves the power of uplifting and inspiring the audience".

"Failure or inability to Relate a part to its entirety might make it inharmonious and incomprehensible to the spectator".

Michael Chekhov, To the Actor,
Routledge, revised 2002, courtesy of the
Michael Chekhov Estate

Michael Chekhov believed that every moment onstage, any role – small or large – deserves to be a work of art unto itself, and that every moment can incorporate ease, form, beauty, and wholeness.

Working with these traits, known as the "Four Brothers", will increase our ability to communicate more specifically via chosen forms, more artistically by cultivating your sense of beauty, more fully and completely by incorporating entirety, and having a sense of ease through it all will benefit you and make your work a pleasure to observe. After all, aren't many drawn to acting because in viewing performances they seem so easy? Of course many discover when dedicating themselves to the craft of acting that it's not always easy, but the aim is to have it appear that way.

Improvisation 1

Part 1: The chairs

Each participant is instructed to bring a chair out into the space, which ideally has room for everyone to move freely. The instructor should then demonstrate moving the chair with a sense of ease, the first of the Four Brothers. Even though the chair has bulk and weight, the focus must be on moving with a sense of ease. Acting is pretending after all, and everyone is now instructed to believe they can move the chair with ease and proceed. Side-coach the participants to be sure their entire body has a sense of ease and that they explore different physical levels…bringing the chair up in the air, bringing it and your body close to the floor. Improvise all the myriad of ways that you can move in relation to the chair, all while focusing on embodying a sense of ease. This is a physical exercise but also a mind exercise – allowing your thoughts to have ease even while you are performing what may be a challenging task. You begin to experience the mind/body connection, working together in harmony to experience ease.

Part 2

After spending some time working with this concept of ease, participants are then instructed to continue moving the chair, but the focus changes. Move the chair with a focus on beauty. This focus is artistic beauty and recognizing that beauty is truly in the eye of the beholder and that we have control over our perception. Now it's time to perceive all aspects of the chair and the way we move the chair and our bodies in relation to the chair and in relation to the space with beauty. If you notice a piece of old gum stuck to the chair bottom, find the beauty in it. Perhaps it's the color of that gum or the free-form shape it's making that is beautiful. The actor can experience artistic beauty internally, and let that beauty radiate out physically, so again body and mind work in harmony. Continue working with the focus on experiencing beauty with you and the chair.

Part 3

The next Brother to focus on is that of form. Be aware of the form of the chair, the form of your own body which changes as you move, and the form you make in relation to the space you are in. Again, explore forms that reach up high and those that are close to the floor. Be sure to be very aware that your body is part of the form that you make with the chair. The form is also part of the entire space in which you are working.

Part 4

Finally, you will focus on a sense of wholeness or entirety. While you continue to work with the chair, imagine your starting point – prior to you moving at all, then the moves that happen will be the middle, and then you come to some sort of conclusion. Hold that concluding moment for three beats, then start all over again. The sustaining of your final moment is excellent training in being able to maintain a specific energy, which in the future will allow your audience a moment to receive what you are depicting onstage. This can be especially helpful when you end an audition piece, to have a short pause to let your work resonate with the auditors, before you break to say thank you. Continue creating these short pieces of art with the chair, with each one being a brief but full event.

Part 5

Now that you have worked with your chair in the space experiencing the Four Brothers on your own it's time to work as part of the ensemble with the entire group. Each individual continues working with their chair, moving with ease, but now the focus is extended beyond your own experience of ease and instead you move with ease amidst the entire group. Don't remain on the perimeter but seek to interact – silently. Everyone will be moving with their chair, and you will extend your consciousness so that you are able to sense all of those around you, and how you are all contributing to this sense of ease – despite moving a challenging object.

The ensemble work continues changing the focus to one "Brother" at a time. Next, move with all the other participants sharing the focus on beauty, then on form – creating shapes now as a group, then on wholeness/entirety – starting and ending with others around you. As this is improvisational, go with the flow. Perhaps you exchange a chair with someone, or groups within the whole may occur and then disband. Remember that you are working as one entire ensemble so there's always an awareness of the entire group.

The finale of this exercise is to have all Four Brothers in mind – moving with ease, having an artistic eye of beauty with how you are moving, being aware of the forms you are making, and then with a group consciousness, coming together in one final sculpture made up of all the chairs and all the participants in the group. Be sure that your awareness extends out to everyone and if one person is still in motion, then everyone should support that colleague by also being in motion until there is an unspoken group decision to come to the final moment of wholeness. This is a great time for an instructor/leader to snap a photo and share with the participants who can then see what the group as a whole created.

Discussion/Reflection

Were you able to focus on each individual "Brother" as you related to the chair? Did you find ease even with the weight of the chair? Did you find any beauty related to the chair that surprised you? Did your awareness of form increase? Did you feel successful in creating bits of art when finding entirety and wholeness by having a specific beginning, middle, and end? Were you able to expand your focus out to the entire group when working as an ensemble? Do you feel the group organically came to a concluding sculpture as a team? What stumbling blocks did you encounter during the improvisation and what ideas might you have to overcome those?

Improvisation 2: The Four Brothers and *you*

Now that you have experienced the Four Brothers with the chairs, it's time to incorporate these into your own being. Hopefully you experienced the ease, beauty, form, and sense of wholeness as you worked with the chair, but sometimes simply moving as you, without a prop, can be a challenge. Start to walk in the space now and initially focus on a sense of ease. Allow yourself to feel comfortable as you walk, and comfortable with everyone that is around you. Even if you feel a bit uneasy, or "on display", simply pretend that you have a sense of ease – and soon it will happen. Next start to think about your own form – your posture, the shapes you make in space as you move through it, then imagine all your movements as a work of art – incorporating beauty. Try various actions in the room such as sitting, getting up, leaning, and picking up and putting down objects. Allow all of these actions to be a little piece of art. Continuing with ease, beauty, and form, add in a sense of wholeness or entirety. As you are moving, choose a destination point. Move to that point incorporating the Four Brothers of Art and once there, hold for a three count to truly establish that sense of completion. Then determine a new destination and perhaps an action – will you pick up an item, sit, lean? Begin your action and when complete, once again hold for a silent count of three to finish with a clear sense of entirety.

Discussion/Reflection

How did you feel incorporating the Four Brothers into your own self and your movement? How was this similar or different from working with chairs? Did you feel you could incorporate all the Brothers at once when you began adding destinations/actions and bringing that activity to a definite conclusion? Did the silent count of three help you to feel a sense of wholeness? How might you use these in other areas of performance?

Improvisation 3: The dancing puppets (duos/trios)

This exercise provides a way for participants to physicalize Michael Chekhov's concepts of ease, form, beauty, and entirety/wholeness, with the premise being that these "Four Brothers" should be in every artistic endeavor.

Clean blindfolds are needed, which could be strips of cloth, or the "sleeping masks" sometimes given out on planes, will work quite well too. Music suitable for classical dance will also be needed, though the genre of music could certainly vary.

Participants divide into teams of two. It is decided between them who will be the puppet and who will be the puppeteer. Explain that puppeteers will be giving the puppet the physical stimulus to move, with perhaps a touch under the arm or behind the knee, or a lift to the foot, with the puppet being blindfolded. Allow the team to consult with each other as to the comfort level of the puppet, so that any sensitive areas are revealed and there is an understanding that only the areas that the puppet expresses comfort with will be touched. If physical touch is a challenge, another way to do this exercise is to have the puppeteer use a pool noodle, stiffened with a dowel, to provide the impulses to the puppet. This worked exceptionally well during the pandemic when touch had to be avoided. Puppets are given the direction to take the impulse that is given and allow themselves to move freely, with a sense of ease and artistic beauty, knowing they are also creating forms from those impulses. Once the puppets and puppeteers are clear on the directions and have made their choices regarding physical touch, puppets are blindfolded and talking ceases. Music is now introduced, and the puppet begins to dance with the impulses given by the puppeteer. The instructor can occasionally side-coach, making sure all body parts are in motion, with cues as needed, such as "are there impulses you can give for the feet...the head...the elbows...etc.". After a time, the instructor coaches the puppeteers to bring their puppets into a duet or a trio. This is where the element of form becomes more apparent, as the puppeteers guide their puppets to work in unison, creating a beautiful form, always with ease. To incorporate the fourth Brother of entirety or wholeness, puppeteers are asked to bring the puppets into a final pose, aware of beauty and form, and again, moving them with ease. Puppeteers should once again be cognizant of their puppet's comfort level, so the physical interaction between puppets stays within the boundaries that have been established. Once the puppets have found their final pose, they are asked to sustain it, and then puppeteers can help puppets remove the blindfolds, so they are able to see where they ended up – always a fun reveal. Partners then change roles so that they each get to experience being both the puppet and puppeteer. Following the exercise, a discussion reveals how each individual experienced the Four Brothers. Part of the discussion often reveals too whether someone was comfortable as the puppet releasing control, or much more comfortable as the puppeteer, being in control. This information is always helpful for an actor to know their natural tendencies, so they can allow that tendency to transform as needed for characters. The exercise gives a visceral experience of Michael Chekhov's Four Brothers of Art, allowing the actor to be aware of incorporating these into other work.

Discussion/Reflection

Did you feel more at ease in one role over the other, puppet vs. puppeteer and if so, why? As the puppet were you able to release into ease and let form be created from the impulses you were given? As the puppeteer, were you able to envision form as you gave those impulses? Were you feeling a sense of entirety and wholeness as the puppet dance concluded?

Improvisation 4: The costume relay race (teams)

This improvisation will allow the participants to work in teams to accomplish a goal, all the while being sure to incorporate the Four Brothers of Art.

The group is divided into two teams and each team is given a similar array of costume items: shirt, jacket, skirt, hat, gloves, perhaps one shoe, vest, tie, scarf – the more colorful and ridiculous the more fun it will be.

When "Go!" is called, each team begins to dress one of their team members and must use every costume piece as it is intended to be worn. If a shirt is too small, then perhaps only one arm goes through a sleeve and the rest hangs. If a shoe is too small, perhaps only the toes are in the shoe and the participant hobbles to the finish line. Once each actor is dressed, they must travel across the room, touch an established point, and then travel back. Simple you say? Adding a task is what can make this even more fun and challenge the team's sense of ease, use of form, ability to always see the beauty, and finish the race with that sense of entirety and wholeness.

Ideas for challenges

Each actor, after being dressed, must bounce a ball up and off a tennis racket for a specified number of times on the way down and on the way back; an actor may be blindfolded and teammates can only use sounds to keep the blindfolded actor on the track both up and back, being sure that the blindfolded team member taps the mid-point and end-point; to make the blindfolded version even more difficult set up chairs or mats on edge and, again, the teammates use sound to guide them. If one is touched, they must return to the start point and begin again. If you really want a challenge and have a floor that's easily cleaned, have the actor balance a raw egg on a spoon. If the egg drops, they must return to the start and the team must clean up the egg before they can begin again. Be creative with your own challenges! If time is limited, rather than traveling up and back to the start, the team can follow the actor down to the end of the space, and then the next person will be dressed and take the return journey, continuing until each person has had a turn. The teams are competing to see who can finish first – though it's all for fun! Be sure to emphasize safety in whatever version is used. If there are obstacles, be sure the blindfolded participant knows that their teammates will be sidecoaching them around those obstacles, so everyone stays safe!

Discussion/Reflection

Were you able to maintain ease even though you were in a race and faced numerous obstacles? Did you feel a sense of entirely and wholeness as everyone completed their task? Were you aware of the varied forms – from each individual in costume to the form needed to complete the relay? Did you find beauty in the absurdity of your costumed peers?

Improvisation 5: Following a plan

For this exercise the leader will place objects in the performance space such as a chair, a table, and some props. The leader will then model a pattern with a sense of wholeness – a beginning and an end, while establishing form with actions. An example would be the leader steps into the space to begin, picks up a book, walks to the chair, opens the book, places the book down to the left of the chair, rises up from the chair and rushes out of the performance space opposite to where they entered. The task is now for each participant to follow this pattern, thereby working with form as is necessary via blocking in a theatre production. You will have a sense of wholeness/entirety with the beginning and ending, and in between create with artistic beauty and a sense of ease.

Discussion/Reflection

How successful were you in recreating the form you were given? Were you able to maintain a sense of ease even if you forgot some of the exact form? Were you able to maintain an improvisational quality, remaining present in the moment, while fulfilling the prescribed actions? Did you sense a feeling of wholeness and entirety with your beginning and ending? Were you able to create with a sense of artistry? Did each participant's creative individuality result in subtle differences even while completing the same tasks? What challenges did you encounter and how might you overcome them next time?

Improvisation 6: Imagining and then following a plan

The same set up as above could be maintained, with several items in the performance space. Now, time is given to the participants so each of them individually decide where their beginning will occur, where they will end, and what they will do in between. This is not spoken or shared. Now, one at a time, each participant will go up to the performance space and fulfill what they imagined, being sure to incorporate the Four Brothers.

Discussion/Reflection

Did you successfully fulfill what you imagined? If not, what happened, and why do you think something changed? Were you able to maintain your feeling of ease even though there was no physical rehearsal, and you were moving through the space with your imagined plan for the first time? Did you feel you applied your sense of artistic beauty to your actions? Did you have a clear beginning and end? For viewers – did a particular story come through from what you witnessed?

Improvisation 7: A-maze-ing objectives with BEEF (contributed by Lisa Dalton, Professional Actor/Director/Educator, Co-Founder and President of NMCA)

This game helps actors understand the nature of objective, obstacles, and storytelling while calling upon the artist to engage Feelings of Beauty, Ease, Entirety and Form (BEEF).

Divide your group into lines of four to eight, depending on the size of the group and the space. Gather at one end of the space and establish a "threshold" line behind which they are all standing. Imagine each group has their own "alley". You ideally want the actors to be able to walk 25–30 feet forward and then return to the end of their line.

For each group, place one light weight object that will lie at rest unless touched, perhaps a crumpled piece of scrap paper, about 20–25 feet from the start line.

The "objective" is for the actors, one at a time to go to the "target" and touch it. The game unfolds by increasing the obstacles to completing this task. How you build the obstacles can vary depending on your time, etc. From the perspective of BEEF, each change of the form of the obstacles, affects the feeling of ease, may be perceived as ugly rather than beautiful and changes the feeling of the whole.

1. NO obstacle (optional): Each person walks to the object, bends down, and touches it with a hand.
2. NO sight: Each person walks to the target with eyes closed and bends down and touches it with hand. Once the hand touches anything (floor, target, obstacle) the actor opens their eyes to assess where they are. Use the last two actors of each line as protectors on either side of their alley for the blind walker. Walkers must walk with eyes closed, with purpose and clarity, and stop and place their hands on the object without hesitation. Protectors stay as quiet and unobtrusive as possible, ready to touch the blind actor in a predetermined safe spot should they get too near danger. The person who has just completed their effort replaces a protector and the protector returns to the end of the line.
3. NO sight, with tempo/rhythm changes. Same as above but blind actors must run as fast as they can. Repeat and go as super slow-motion/inner stillness as they can. Repeat with skipping lyrically, chaotically, staccato, Legato.
4. NO sight with Set Pieces. Building from above, add in various boxes, books, blankets, random, (not too dangerous) objects to create a maze through which they must go, blindly. If they touch any object with any part of their body or clothes, their turn is done, they switch to be protectors, etc.

Discussion/Reflection

Check in at various times for what they are learning and observing. Is someone peeking? Is it interesting or boring and obvious when they are? Which ones are most interesting? The perfect ones, those that get really close and miss or the ones that are so far off yet really trying? What is happening to the atmosphere? Who lost their feeling of ease? How did their feeling of ease affect their form? Their enjoyment of the whole? What happened to the actor's and audience's breathing when the actor was in trouble? Were there beautiful moments? What else?

Tricks to watch for

Some actors will try to count steps. Is this interesting? Try changing the position of the object. An actor hovering over the area without committing to playing their hand down is a "violation of the feeling of the whole/lacking commitment" and may be called out. Actors who try to touch the object with their feet surreptitiously before reaching for it are called out. Make sure no floor surface changes make counting steps easy. Move obstacles into new positions that always block a straight path to the target. The number of actors in each group should ideally be enough to have several waiting and watching in line and at least two protectors. Two protectors can also be referees and call out an actor.

Wrap up

Move chairs (or other chosen object) with ease, beauty, form and wholeness/entirety. Once this is achieved individually, share these points of concentration with the entire group, eventually creating a final sculpture.

- Dancing Puppets: A blindfolded "puppet" is given movement cues from a puppeteer and together they create a dance of artistic beauty with ease and form, eventually forming a duet or trio to complete a sense of wholeness.
- Costume Relay: Two teams dress one person at a time and that person makes the journey as determined and then the next person goes until one team finishes first. Make this more complex by adding a task.

Follow a plan: Whether provided or imagined, use your sense of form, ease, artistic beauty, and wholeness to execute a piece of art.

Solo application

As you may have deduced from the exercises above, much of this work can be done solo and allow you to experience the freedom that incorporating these Brothers can provide to you. You may be working at home and don't have the space to manipulate a chair, but you can apply these to any object. When working on your own, apply these to an everyday action such as brushing your teeth which will allow you to discover these "Brothers" of art in a naturalistic way. Or simply move through space on your own and allow yourself to focus on one Brother at a time and then amalgamate them into other simple actions that you perform.

Script application

While any role may require challenges, approach these with ease as an artist, knowing that you are imbuing your work with artistic beauty. This does not mean you'll never create despicable characters but paint them with the beauty of art that allows an audience a deeper understanding of them. As for form, you may note in the margins of your script your physical actions, from entrances and exits to basic stage business, creating a score for yourself. Even when alone, rehearsing your lines along with doing the actions can marry them together and allow you to deepen your memory and comfort level – increasing your sense of ease. Find the beginnings and endings, not only for the entire piece of work, but for smaller segments. Remember that a poignant pause can help solidify an ending moment.

Life application

As you may imagine, applying these Four Brothers in your life can lead to amazing freedom. Imagine being in a frustrating situation but then remembering "ease" and applying it in that moment. Being aware of form can allow you to carry yourself and perform actions with intention, confidence and grace, and to work toward your most advantageous form whether that be for bowling, tennis, or dance. Actors are consistently auditioning, but even if you are not an actor you may be interviewing for jobs, or meeting someone new, and incorporating the Brothers in these circumstances can dispel the stress of these unknown situations. Imagining beauty in all that you see and experience, from that gum stuck to the bottom of the chair to a traffic jam, can certainly assist with creating more ease in your life and appreciation for whatever presents itself to you. Using the idea of wholeness/entirety can allow you to employ closures in order to then make new and clear beginnings – cycling through your days with more clarity of purpose. Even just breathing with a sense of ease, form, beauty, and entirety can induce a sense of calmness and control.

FIGURE 3.1 Four actors standing still at varied levels surround the fifth actor. Photograph by Melis Derya White. Actors from L to R: Arleth Lopez, Luis Alfonso Castro, Shawn Pirkle, Aslan Longoria, Omar Moreno

3

QUALITIES OF MOVEMENT

MOLDING, FLOWING, FLYING, AND RADIATING

> "[S]ay to yourself: 'Every movement I make is a little piece of art, I am doing it like an artist... Through my body I am able to convey to the spectator my inner power and strength'".
>
> "You will develop a taste for form and will be artistically dissatisfied with any movements that are vague and shapeless, or with amorphous gestures, speech, thoughts, feelings and will impulses when you encounter them in yourself and others during your professional work".
>
> Michael Chekhov, To the Actor,
> Routledge, Revised 2002, courtesy of the
> Michael Chekhov Estate

Haven't we all had a fantasy or even a very realistic dream of flying? In this chapter flying is one of the tools which will be explored to bring about transformation in any performance. Michael Chekhov referred to these tools as movement qualities. Beginning with the strongest resistance in movement, which is molding, and gradually moving toward radiating, which is energy having no bounds, you will be introduced to a full range of movement that allows for a variety of expression. When improvising with these tools you may choose a character that is very regimented and controlled via molding, or a character that is very free and expressive via flying. As with the other Michael Chekhov acting techniques, these tools hold neither a positive nor negative charge, but instead offer physical ways of being with endless possibilities. A discovery can be made via these tools which is that any character you will ever play can move somewhere on this spectrum – or incorporate the entire range!

Qualities of movement – mold, flow, fly, and radiate relate to Earth, Water, Air, and Light, and provide the actor with a range of ways to move and speak. Improvisation samples include moving with props, with chairs, and as inventors sharing ideas. Recognize that all of these qualities can be experienced with varied tempo and intensity. Earth may be stone or clay, water may be still or a rushing river, air may be a light breeze or a tornado, and light may be sunny warmth or fire. Eventually choosing these qualities will depend upon your analysis of your character and your script.

Improvisation 1

Each individual finds their own spot within the space, as this improvisation begins by working solo. Begin in a universal stance and imagine that you are encased in rock, but you have the ability to mold that rock, to carve and sculpt it, although there will still be plenty of resistance. Now focus on moving with the quality of molding, more than the miming of the rock – the idea of rock provides you with an initial image, but now you can focus on the resistance, and how that movement feels in the body. While you are molding, starting first with just the hands and fingers and slowly the rest of the body, be aware of any feelings that arise. Is this movement awakening a certain urge or desire? Is this movement creating a certain state of mind for you, or evoking a certain sensation? Perhaps any sensation you are experiencing may also evoke a certain feeling? Be sure to be very precise with this molding. If your eyes change where they are focusing, be sure you are molding your eyes to that new spot. If you take a step, be sure to mold each separate movement of that step, from toes through to the heel. Now once you've focused on molding through stone, let that stone change to clay. There is still plenty of resistance to clay, but it is easier to carve and sculpt than stone. Again, check in with the feelings and images that arise as you allow your entire body to move in abstract ways with this molding quality. Be sure to explore a variety of levels and directions. Now let yourself mold out the numbers with your voice, from one to ten. Be sure all the mechanisms of articulation are molding…molding the jaw as it opens, and the tongue and lips as they move to make sound. Don't judge what sound comes out, just be sure you are molding that sound – it's all perfect.

Next, allow some water to seep into the clay so that it becomes mud. Now the resistance is less, though still palpable. Continue moving in large abstract ways as the sculptor, molding your way in the space. Imagine more and more water enters and surrounds you so that now you are moving with a flowing quality.* (You'll note that this is also one of Rudolph Laban's movement qualities and it is known that Michael Chekhov and Rudolph Laban were teaching at the same time at Dartington Hall in England, during the late 1930's.) Allow yourself to freely flow through the entire space, recognizing that water still has some resistance so that needs to determine the quality of your movement. Continue to explore levels and directions. Be aware of feelings and images that arise for you.

Next imagine the water around you starts to flow more rapidly, becoming a rushing river. Continue to move with that flowing quality but now at a faster tempo. Imagine that the river you are part of now tumbles over a waterfall and evaporates into the air, and your movement quality now becomes one of flying. You are one with the air around you and able to soar around the space. When working with an ensemble be sure to retain your awareness of others so there aren't any collisions. If you do realize you are heading into a direct connection, simply spin to another clear direction before you meet up. Enjoy all the varied elements of flying. From your entire body flying across the room to hovering and allowing an arm to fly up into the air, or a leg to fly left or back – so many variations. As before, check in with any images or feelings that may arise.

Next imagine that you continue to fly higher into the sky and you are headed toward a beautiful blazing sun. You collide and merge with that sun and the sun's intensity of light, so you are now radiating fire. Imagine fiery energy in every cell of your body, radiating out of every pore in all directions. Explore the way your body radiates this fiery energy. Lift a knee and acknowledge how that kneecap radiates the energy of fire. Imagine that fire behind your eyes as you view the space. Imagine that fire in the tips of your fingers as you send those fingers in various directions. Every part of you is radiating this fire. Let that fire build to laser beams which radiate from every part of you. Allow sound to come out as you shoot those laser rays all around the space, radiating in all directions – through the floor and through the ceiling and walls. Next imagine that energy morphs into a more calm, radiant sun – the kind you may experience on a warm beach. Your energy is still radiating, but now each cell is filled with warm sunshine which comes through every pore. That warm sunny radiance is behind your eyes, and in the sole of your foot with each step you take. It's in the palms of your hands and runs up and down your spine. You are a radiant being moving through the space.

Discussion/Reflection

What did molding, flowing, flying, and radiating create for you? There's no right or wrong as all this work allows the individual to amalgamate their own storehouse of images and reactions from these techniques, to then be utilized when applied to a performance. Perhaps molding allowed you to feel more precise and exacting. Did a character image form from those feelings? What sort of character might be more precise and exacting? Perhaps the molding brought up feelings of frustration and being trapped. How could you use that in a future performance? How about flowing? Did it allow you to embody the motto "go with the flow"? Perhaps flowing is not a typical movement for you and felt foreign. How about flying? Did you find freedom? Did it remind you of a type of character or even someone or something from life that you could relate to? How about the varying degrees of light? How did you feel when you were radiating fire? Did that conjure up the image of a superhero who is invincible? Perhaps the fire brought about anger or an urge to dominate. What happened when the quality of light changed? Did you feel more of a piercing energy when you were radiating laser beams? Was that your superhero moment? How about radiating the calm, warm sunshine? What character might that be? Did specific feelings arise from this?

The idea behind these movement qualities is that any character may be somewhere in this range, from the slowest molding to the most intense radiating, and may go through variations during the arc of their journey in a story. Perhaps your character is very bureaucratic and enjoys precision and rules. Using a molding quality could assist you with creating the physical life of this character, complete with molding gestures and perhaps words that are molded with precision. You may play a very easy-going yoga instructor and need to flow through your scenes, until a conflict arises and this same character flies into a rage, only to then realize the low level of importance to the conflict and they regain their composure, realizing how foolish they were and radiate warm sunshine.

Improvisation 2: Everyday chat (duos/trios)

Working with a partner, choose a topic of discussion. You could be in a circle and each person facing a partner, or randomly spread in the space. You will be working in teams of two, or with three as needed depending on the number of participants. Your topic could be a vacation, or what to prepare for a meal, or how to celebrate a holiday. One actor will travel through molding to radiating discussing this topic, and the other actor can only say "Yes" or "No". The actor discussing the topic allows those yes and no responses to spin them into another quality. You don't want to predetermine what any quality will be – simply authentically react and allow your voice and body to follow suit. An example may be that one partner starts molding and being very prescriptive about what they want and how everything should be, then maybe a "Yes" is heard and they begin to flow as they feel their ideas being accepted. Perhaps a "No" inspires them to fly with frustration and then they hear a "Yes" and they radiate warm sunshine of appreciation because their idea was again accepted and then another "No" and they shoot lasers of hostility at their partner. As a sample and depending upon the skill of the participants, the instructor may choose to call out these specific reactions to demonstrate the possibilities. Then once participants are more comfortable with how they can switch from one quality to the next, a more free-form improvisation can ensue. There is never a positive or negative charge given to any of these qualities. You can fly with utter joy or mold with icy coldness. Let the improvisation be whatever it will be, knowing there is no right or wrong.

Discussion/Reflection

How did you feel when responding to the "Yes" or "No"? How did using the various qualities allow your reactions to vary? If you were observing the changes in movement qualities, what feelings seemed to be displayed? Did a certain story emerge for you?

Improvisation 3: Hello and goodbye

Like the last improvisation, this can be done in a circle with two volunteers, each being given a quality with which to enter the circle. They turn their backs to the circle and focus on bringing that quality back and then when the leader claps, into the circle they go with a simple conversation: "Hello" – "Hi" – "How are you?" – "Fine, how about you?" – "Fine" – "I've got to go" – "I've got to go too".

This can result in some terrific examples of how these qualities can create character instantly and inspire varied feelings. A character may be molding, giving them a veneer of not caring and not being interested while the character they interact with may be flying and full of fun and joy and wanting to share that with someone. This also points out how conflict, a typical part of any story, can be a result of disparate personalities interacting.

Discussion/Reflection

Even though it wasn't shared, did you notice which one of the qualities was being used? What kind of feeling did each character exude as a result of using the movement quality? How did these affect the interactions? Who did you imagine the two characters were to one another?

Improvisation 4: Invention convention

A table on props is established in the playing area. Each participant picks up one of these props. They are now the inventor of this prop which can have a myriad of uses well beyond whatever the typical use of this item would be. A spatula can not only flip pancakes, but can be a fly swatter, a shoehorn for those with wide feet, and glancing at the shiny flat surface, a hypnosis device. There is no limit as to what each actor's imagination can create. Now, each inventor needs to convince others to invest in his/her/their product – that it is the best of this year's convention. The participants begin improvising but they must do this with the quality of molding. Side-coaching by the leader should include reminding them that the entire body must be molding, from the top of the head to the toes and that the molding quality now extends into the prop and how it is moved. The speech must also be molding. Every sound should be precise with attention to sculpting the sounds out of the mouth. Next the group is instructed to flow, then fly, then radiate fire, radiate lasers, and finally to radiate warm sunshine. All the while they must keep their intention of trying to sell others on their product. When a new movement quality is called, the same dialogue continues, but now changes due to the new energy. Once everyone has been able to experience all of these within the improvisation, they now are given numbers. Number 1 begins molding and then moves through the four qualities up to radiating. Number 2 begins with flowing, number 3 with flying, and number 4 with radiating fire. Now the improvisation has varied dynamics as the inventors once again meet up with characters who behave very differently than they do. At the sound of a clap, bell, whistle or simply calling out the instruction: "Switch", each participant moves onto the next movement quality in the sequence. Those who are molding now move onto flowing, those flowing move to flying, and those that are flying now radiate. The radiating characters may switch to fire, or lasers, or another form of light within the radiating quality, such as warm sunshine. With a large group the improvisation can get quite loud and animated, so having a bell or whistle can help the leader protect their own voice and not have to shout! The joy of improvisation – there is no right or wrong, it's art! At some point the inventors are called to a circle. They remain moving with whichever quality they were recently in. The leader now goes to each inventor and asks them to vote on which item they feel is the star of this year's invention convention. Perhaps they feel it is their own, but whatever the choice it's then fun to hear what came up during the improv and to see these characters speak individually for a moment.

Discussion/Reflection

Which of the movement qualities felt more comfortable to you and why? Was one quality more in line with your typical way of being? How did others convince you that their product was the best? Did using a movement quality assist you in pursuing your objective?

NOTE: For all the improvisations, character names should be used and never the actor's name. The point of all these exercises is transformation, to transcend your everyday self and enter a level of artistry, of imaginative creativity, and finding a character name is part of that process.

Improvisation 5: Diverse duos pursue objectives

The focus of this improvisation is for each character to pursue the shared objective with their partner but pursuing that with the specific movement quality given. This allows for the all-important connection to an objective that happens in any well-written script, approaching the pursuit of that objective in a defined way. Depending on the size of the group and the time available, teams could spread around the room, and all improvise the same scene, or a team can present in front of the group, with all contributing to the discussion after viewing. If everyone is working at once, "Freeze" can be called so others can then watch an individual scene, then move on to another so that everyone can have a bit of time to share what they are improvising.

Scenario 1

A "molding" architect and a "flying" architect have been charged with designing a celebrity's home in the Hollywood Hills. The duo can decide on who the celebrity is which may inform the improv. While truthfully pursuing the objective of creating the design, the two architects remain with their movement qualities, also allowing those qualities to inform their voice and delivery of their ideas.

Scenario 2

A "flowing" character and a "radiating fire" character are business partners opening a fitness studio. The improvisation can revolve around what sort of fitness they will offer, and the duo works to pursue a defined plan as they maintain these diverse qualities.

(Many more scenarios can be created with these serving as examples. A team pursues a common objective but approaches that objective with different movement qualities and the improvisation often unfolds in very fun and surprising ways.)

Discussion/Reflection

Though it was not given, did conflict arise due to the diverse movement qualities assigned? Were the characters able to resolve their conflicts if so, and how? Was the objective clearly pursued? Were the characters able to maintain their individual movement qualities even when quite different from their scene partner?

Improvisation 6: Animal and creature work (contributed by Paul Hurley, Professional Actor, Associate Professor of Acting and Movement at Kent State University, and Certified Teacher via NMCA)

A wonderful way to explore this tool in a playful improvisation is to invite the performers to allow each of the four Qualities of Movement to inspire the creation of either an animal or a fantastical creature. Animals are often a great place to start, as this activity encourages each person to use their imagination to take on a being that already exists (such as a *molding* sloth or a *flying* gazelle). Once everyone has explored an animal, the next step could be to transform into other-worldly or mythical creatures. These can be creatures that have been already defined (dragons, centaurs, fairies, etc.), creatures from fantasy novels/games (along the lines of Lord of the Rings, D&D, etc.), or they could be creatures that are newly created in the imagination of the performer using each quality as the inspiration.

The first part of this improvisational animal/creature work can be structured to give the performers a few minutes to explore each of the following:

- MOLDING creatures/animals
- FLOWING creatures/animals
- FLYING creatures/animals
- RADIATING creatures/animals

For the second part of this improvisation, divide all the performers into four groups and assign each group to a specific quality of movement (the performer can either revisit one of their past creations or develop a new one for this exercise). In this subsequent exploration, there will now be creatures and/or animals from all four of the Qualities of Movement interacting with one another, and many fun and interesting encounters will occur. Perhaps alliances and relationships are formed, or perhaps factions are created. As the facilitator of the improvisation, you can prompt the group to explore and engage in a variety of interactions.

The beauty of this improvisation is that it allows each performer to utilize their imagination to experience each of the Qualities of Movement with an unveiled and unleashed physicality.

Improvisation 7: Waiting for the bus (contributed by Paul Hurley, Professional Actor, Associate Professor of Acting and Movement at Kent State University, and Certified Teacher via NMCA)

If the first improvisation was completely unveiled, this next improvisation will explore veiling each of the Qualities of Movement. Have two performers sit or stand side by side, as if they were waiting for a bus. Give each performer a quality (Person A is radiating and Person B is flowing). The performers will then improvise a scene using only their head. In this improvisation all kinds of wonderful circumstances, relationships, and encounters will emerge. This can be a fun exercise for pairs to go individually while the rest of the group observes. Another possible progression to this improv is to include an additional body part for each performer (for example, Person A can only use their head and right arm, and Person B can only use their head and chest).

In Chapter 11, I will share how the Qualities of Movement can be further layered into improvisational explorations of the Thinking, Feeling, and Willing psychological forces.

Wrap up

Explore the four movement qualities of molding, flowing, flying, and radiation, experimenting with the variety of ways each can be expressed. Molding can be rock or clay, flowing can be serene water or a rushing river, flying can be gliding or rocketing, and radiating can range from warm sunshine to fire. Improvise with the tools and discover the ways these can create unique characters and specific ways to pursue objectives.

QUALITIES OF MOVEMENT

Solo application

When working solo with these, give yourself a simple action, such as retrieving a book from a table, but see how your action changes when you mold to the book, fly away once you have retrieved the book, etc., and what story that might tell.

Script application

When reviewing a script, determine when your character may be molding and moving in a very deliberate way due to the objective being pursued and when they may be flying – perhaps due to a strong emotional reaction to an incident, or when they might be flowing or radiating. These could be character attributes or the way a character pursues their intentions. Throughout the story being told, you can create a score of these movement qualities, allowing a throughline for your character that is filled with variety and nuance.

Life application

At times it may be very wise to approach an activity with a molding quality to be precise and careful with a sensitive task. You may realize that your current energy is at a molding level, but you need to rise up and fly in order to achieve something requiring a faster approach. Flowing may be a wonderful state for you to induce to remain calm and not allow whatever might be happening to affect you in a negative way. For a presentation, you may choose to radiate warm sunshine to your viewers or spew a bit of fire to make a strong point. Being aware of these four movement qualities and putting them to use can strengthen your communication in any arena. You may realize that in life you function primarily with one quality, but you can notice how in certain situations the other qualities come into play and you can use them to strengthen your communication and connection to others.

FIGURE 4.1 One actor (center) pushing forward, with four actors in surrounding positions. Photograph by Melis Derya White. Actors from L to R: Shawn Pirkle, Luis Alfonso Castro, Omar Moreno, Arleth Lopez, Aslan Longoria

4
ARCHETYPAL GESTURES

> *"There are two kinds of gestures. One we use both while acting on the stage and in everyday life – the natural and usual gesture. The other kind is what might be called the archetypal gesture, one which serves as an original model for all possible gestures of the same kind".*
>
> Michael Chekhov, To the Actor,
> Routledge, Revised 2002, courtesy of the
> Michael Chekhov Estate

Dictionary.com provides the definition of archetypal as: "adjective: perfect or typical as a specimen of something; being an original model or pattern or a prototype". This chapter will reveal ten archetypal gestures, as introduced in the training by NMCA, allowing for you to experience what may be primal within you and to expand your movement options. From pushing to smashing, from lifting to reaching, these movements allow the body and psyche to awaken what may be lost ways in your expression of movement and this work restores all these possibilities for extensive acting choices. Experiencing these will allow us to better relate to any character – or others in life! Whether fully expressed, or more physically subtle, termed as "veiling" by Michael Chekhov, or perhaps even invisible to the observer, these gestures provide a way to express a character's intentions and/or feelings.

During our growing up, we all develop our own unique physicality and become comfortable with certain ways of moving. As a performer, the more flexible you can be, figuratively and literally, the more options you will have when it comes to artistic creation. Practicing archetypal gestures can restore movements that you may not have experienced since you were a young child, thereby giving you access to a wealth of possibilities. NMCA works with ten archetypal gestures, feeling that all these that will be introduced can be helpful. Please note that other practitioners of the Michael Chekhov technique may work with 4 or 6 or 20, but as is repeated several times in this book, that is perfect. The object of any technique is to support your artistry so whatever works best for you is what you should choose. There are often very traditional ways that these are taught, with specific choreography, or they may be practiced with a more freestyle form. Some more specific forms will be provided here but feel free to improvise on these forms to discover what inspires you the most. This is a situation where practice will lead to being more facile with these, until you can simply imagine the gesture and without any movement, receive the impulse that the gesture conjures for you. Once you are familiar with them all, the next improvisation will provide you with qualities to apply to the movements so you can discover the limitless possibilities they hold. After that, improvisational scenarios will let you utilize these gestures as characters in various situations.

Guiding Principle: With all of the gesture work, you'll want to engage your breath. An inhalation will happen as you prepare for the gesture, ideally expanding in a direction opposite to where you will eventually move. You will exhale on the action, and allow that exhalation to last as long as the action continues. In order to have a sense of wholeness, be sure and sustain the final moment of the gesture for several seconds, allowing you to fully experience the charge of each gesture, and then let it go. For the initial work with these gestures, be sure that your entire body is engaged. You will also want to repeat each gesture dozens of times so that you can truly recognize the sensations you receive, and experience how slight variations can alter your experience and perceptions.

Improvisational exercises: Discovering archetypal gestures

Gesture 1: The push

Beginning with your body in a universal stance, with your own best physical alignment, lift your arms up to face level, palms facing front, and take a slight step back while the elbows also reach back. Then allow your front foot to slightly lunge forward, with the palms now pushing in unison to the front. This movement into the space behind you allows you to gather energy in the opposite direction from where you eventually send the energy, thereby providing a preparation. Repeat this over and over again, with the knowledge that you are simply willing yourself to push. Sustain the finale of each push for several seconds, allowing the energy to radiate within and outside of you. This is not a mime, where you imagine pushing a particular object, but instead you simply fulfill the urge to push. As you are repeating this movement, allow your imagination to be open, to reveal what feeling or intention may arise with this movement. Once you are comfortable with the movement, move onto the next so that you will gain the vocabulary of all ten archetypal gestures listed here.

Gesture 2: The pull

From your universal stance, step forward with one foot and both arms outstretched and then let your hands close into a grasp and pull energy toward you and past your body. Your foot can pull in toward you as well so that your sustaining moment will bring your feet back toward your universal stance. You want to be sure that you engage the entire body, from head to toe, in the process. You can experiment with a fully closed grasp, or let your hands be slightly open as you pull, allowing some air. After you pull to one side of the body, pull to the other side. You will then recognize the varied sensations you receive by trying the pull in slightly different ways. Be sure to sustain the energy at the completion of each push, to fully feel the effect.

Gesture 3: The smash

With legs apart, in a ballet style second position and keeping the knees fluid, clasp your hands together in front of you. Let those hands create a semi-circle, lifting to the left or the right, and then let them smash down the center, like a hammer, between the legs – allowing the knees to bend. You may be inspired to let out a sound with this movement – let it fly – just be sure to allow your throat to remain open so there's no strain.

Gesture 4: The lift

From your universal stance, bring one foot slightly forward and bend your knees so that you become closer to the ground, with your open palms also reaching downwards. Then stretch your arms up toward the sky as your legs also stretch to their full length, thereby completing your lift. Your gaze will naturally follow your hands skyward. Sustain that lift, simply allowing whatever sensations are there to radiate for a time, then return to the start and lift again.

Gesture 5: The gather

From universal, let your arms stretch out to either side of you at shoulder height and then bring them together in a gathering movement. You can also let a foot stretch out the side and simultaneously gather with that foot along with the arms. You may experiment with varied tempos to discover a variety of sensations. Sustain the finale of your gathering, no matter what the tempo, to build your awareness of the effect.

Gesture 6: The throw

As a baseball pitcher would do, bring your arm behind you with your hand slightly clenched as if you are holding an imaginary ball of energy and one foot stepping back at the same time. Then throw forward with that arm, stepping into the throw, releasing the energy. Sustain, release, then repeat.

Gesture 7: The reach

While this version still has energy going upwards like the lift, the palms are facing forward and the fingers are extended as you bring your arms up to the sky, and perhaps even rise up on your toes as you fully commit to reaching. Sustain that authentic reach for several seconds, being aware of the movement is influencing you.

Gesture 8: The drag

Imagine energy behind you and you reach your arms back and step one foot back as you take hold of that energy. Then, leading with the center of your chest, drag your foot through the center and then in front of you as you step forward and drag that energy behind you with both hands. Sustain for a few moments after the most active part of the drag to let the energy resonate.

Gesture 9: The penetration

Step backward with one foot while you bring your palms together in front of your chest. Point your fingers forward as you rock on your front foot and bring your joined hands out in front of you to penetrate. You may also experiment with a full step forward as a variation, always being aware of the sensations. Sustain the finale of the penetration, letting the energy penetrate within you and where you are focused.

Gesture 10: The tear

Bring your closed fists to meet in front of your chest, with your feet planted hip distance apart. Next, pull your fists apart with force as you step out to one side, tearing laterally. You can also try multiple directions – tearing from the center high and low, or tearing at a diagonal. Which one provides you with the urgency to tear? Enjoy trying different variations, keeping a keen awareness as to how each one resonates within you. Sustain the end-point of your tear and let the energy radiate.

Improvisation 1: Making discoveries

Now that you have practiced these ten archetypal gestures with a specific form, it's time to improvise and discover forms that energize you. Push and pull in all different directions, smash sideways and behind you, lift with your feet – be creative and have fun with these. Discover what versions of these gestures invigorate you. The goal is to have these movements live in you organically, so that you may call upon them for any scene or character in the future. You may also apply varying qualities to these gestures. Sometimes simply changing the tempo can change the sensation of the gesture – gathering quickly may become greedy or pulling slowly may become flirtatious. You can also directly apply a quality to a gesture – what happens if you smash comically or lift viciously. The very nature of the gesture can change and would certainly be interpreted differently when used as part of a story. By becoming facile with these your repertoire of expression will be vastly increased. The improvisations will begin to allow you to experience how marrying qualities and gestures can create specific intentions.

Improvisation 2: Communicate via veiling

Working with a group, you'll want to make two lines, where participants are facing each other so that you and the person opposite become a team. For this exercise you will now use these gestures to affect your partner, just as you may do when acting in a scene. This will also incorporate Michael Chekhov's concept of veiling. Veiling refers to lessening the physicalizing of an element, in this case the archetypal gesture, but still maintaining the intensity and energy. In Chekhov's time in Hollywood, an obstruction of the motion picture camera lens would tone down a scene, or blur an image, perhaps with the use of Vaseline or other substances.

While Vaseline may have been used in film in days gone by to create a slightly blurred image for the screen, the performers didn't change what they were doing. Similarly, when veiling a gesture, you want to be sure your internal energy does not diminish, only the physical expression, so that the power behind the chosen gesture is still effective.

Ideally a leader will call out the archetypal gesture, such as push. One line will be dedicated to the action, while the opposite line is instructed to simply receive that gesture and the accompanying energy from the partner opposite them. This improvisation is done silently, with a follow-up discussion once finished. Side-coach the sender to fully express the gesture. With the push be sure your legs are involved, and both hands are pushing, and that you are consciously working to affect the partner across from you. A reminder is given that this is not personal, this is for the sake of acting, and the stronger your scene partner is the more you must react too, so you want that strength coming at you. The receiver of the action may move slightly but ideally remains in place, absorbing what is being given to them. Receivers should have the awareness that they are taking in whatever energy is coming toward them. In acting, we all want strong partners that make our job easier, so even if the energy is a bit rough, as a receiver be sure to allow it in. Now the veiling comes into play. The leader now instructs the senders of the push to take the legs out of the gesture – just push with the arms. Once this is established several times, the coaching now becomes: "Push with just one hand". After allowing the one-handed push to occur several times, the instruction now is: "Push with just a finger…don't lose any of the intensity. Internally and energetically, you should feel as if you are still pushing with your entire body." After a few rounds of the finger push, now the leader instructs: "No movement at all now. Just look into your partner's eyes and push them." Oftentimes this may be the most intense, as most of us are familiar with the adage "if looks could kill". This veiling technique is exceptional for on-camera training where a close-up needs to reveal the thoughts and feelings of a character that most often are revealed via the eyes, or perhaps the countenance of the face. Once a few moments of silently sending the push have been completed, the leader instructs everyone to relax and to connect with their partner to discover what happened. How did it feel sending that push and how did it change as the physical movements were veiled? How did the receiver feel? What did the receiver feel was coming at them and what sensation or feeling did they experience as a result?

Next, roles switch, and the partners that were receivers now act. The group works through all ten of the archetypal gestures in this way, beginning with the gesture physicalized through the entire body, and ending with just eye contact, followed up by discussion.

Discussion/Reflection

The discussion should bring to light how powerful these gestures are, and that by simply willing yourself to fully embody them, they can have a strong effect on a partner. It should also become apparent that once mastered, the full physical expression is not necessary, but that simply sending the energy of the chosen gesture through the eyes can communicate strongly.

Improvisation 3: Gestures with intention

In this improvised connection with a partner, participants will now employ a specific intention to their gesture, to show how making choices will influence the way the gesture is perceived, and how it can be employed as a character's tactic. Each gesture will also be experienced in what may be called "opposite ways", so that it becomes apparent that no gesture carries a positive or negative connotation, but rather it is the actor who chooses how they work with each gesture.

For this improv, the participants can remain facing each other in one long line, with each having their own partner, or the leader may choose to have them scatter in teams throughout the space – whichever feels best.

Once again, one of the team members is chosen to take action while the other will receive. The image or intention is written on paper and then shown only to those taking action. Once all the actors have absorbed the intention or image, then they begin, as before, fully expressing the gesture, aiming it at their partner as they want that partner to feel what they have been given to convey. As before, the leader will side-coach them to slowly veil this full gesture, so with the push, first taking out the feet, then using just one arm, just a hand, just a finger, and finally sending that energy via eye contact with their partner.

Below are intentions and images for each archetypal gesture, focused on opposite results with the same gesture, to demonstrate their versatility and the power of making a choice. Eventually the analysis of a script would dictate the best choices for each moment on stage or screen. Once these have been experienced, have fun by making up your own! Below are some oppositional intentions to employ to get started.

- Push: to eliminate, to motivate
- Pull: to the heart with unconditional love, to throw away
- Smash: to annihilate, to launch into success
- Lift: to bolster confidence, to dismiss
- Gather: to embrace, to rob them of dignity
- Throw: to inspire them to reach new heights, to hurl disdain
- Reach: to understand and accept, to force a solution
- Drag: to bring them along with you, to move them out of your superior path
- Penetrate: to connect with their highest thoughts, to manipulate their thoughts
- Tear: to rid them of their problems, to rip them to shreds

Thinking about stage and screen productions you have seen, you can probably relate all of these to characters in those productions, and their objectives. The possibilities of motivation are endless, but when connected to these archetypal gestures, you have a way to physicalize them – whether full-bodied for a highly physicalized stage production such as a farce or use them in a very subtle way for a camera close-up with the energy concentrated in the eyes.

Discussion/Reflection

Did the gestures assist with the given intention? Were you able to use the physicality of the gesture to better feel the intention? When reducing the gesture down to being fully veiled, could you still sustain the energy of the gesture and intention within you?

Improvisation 4: Speed dating

This improv is based on "speed dating" and typically results in much fun for the participants, and anyone observing. As in previous improvisations, there are two lines of participants though this is much easier if everyone is seated in a chair. The leader will ring a bell or chime for the dating to commence, and ring again when it is time to switch. When the switch happens, one designated line all moves in one direction, with the person at the very end of the chairs rotating to the front of the line. Each potential date is given one of the archetypal gestures and how that gesture relates to their intention which becomes their main line of conversation. As participants remain seated, the gestures are now veiled, becoming part of how the characters express themselves as they converse. A push may now be only in the fingers or a pull may just be through the eyes.

Here are examples of what can be given to those in the dating line – though, as before, there are endless possibilities for you to discover on your own.

- Push your dating agenda on them – (what you like to do on a date)
- Push your ideology on them (they should adhere to your values)
- Pull them toward your heart as your character feels an instant connection
- Pull them into a scheme of yours (to make a past date jealous)

- Smash out any insecurities you may sense in them
- Smash to demonstrate how intently you are committed to finding "the one"
- Lift them to lighten their mood
- Lift them to show you admire them
- Gather them to you and show how caring you are
- Gather them because you like to control others
- Throw out a myriad of ideas for upcoming dates
- Throw them a curve ball by throwing out obscure personal information
- Reach into their heart to discover their true desires
- Reach into their mind to assess their level of knowledge
- Penetrate their heart to see if they are truly honest
- Penetrate their thoughts to determine if they are an intellectual match
- Tear them open to force them to be vulnerable
- Tear into their soul to discover their true nature

While many of these listed may seem rather esoteric, you probably realize that a character might have the motivation as listed and the archetypal gestures give you a physical way to pursue these, even if you are uncertain how to go about the listed objective. Sitting for this improvisation will naturally veil the full expression of the archetypal gesture and viewing the subtler renditions of them will remind you how they are present in everyday life.

Discussion/Reflection

Once everyone has been able to chat with each other, the leader rings the bell/chime again to bring it to a close, but then asks each who they'd most like to date and why, with everyone responding in character of course. It's also important that everyone use a character name and not their own – this is not about anyone's individual personality, but instead their improvised personality used for the exercise

Wrap up

Explore the ten archetypal gestures given in various ways, from having very specific form to freestyle, being aware of how you are best energized. Improvise in various ways to discover how you can communicate and pursue objectives by employing these gestures.

Solo application

Observe others around you using these gestures in subtle ways which will allow you to build your physical vocabulary and understand how these relate to intentions. Continue to work on variations of these so you find your own unique ways of movement and expand the ways you can incorporate them into a role.

Script application

These archetypal gestures are an excellent way for you to score your script and inspire action as your character pursues objectives. Rather than thinking about your character's intention, consider how that intention might come through via one of these gestures? Varying the way you physicalize a gesture will give the character's objective specificity, and altering even the same gesture could result in a variation of tactic while pursuing that same objective. Using these you may wind up with a variety of archetypal gestures in the margin of your script creating a score, such as push, then tear, then gather, then reach, which will give you prompts as to what your character is pursuing in those moments and how they are implementing various tactics. These may be strongly revealed or quite veiled, depending on what is appropriate for the material you apply them to.

Life application

Deliberately employing these techniques when communicating in any situation can make that communication more effective, as you wed your gestures with the information you are sharing. Knowing these can help you read others and what their intentions may be, just by viewing gestures that may accompany speech. This can allow you more understanding and empathy. As you experiment with the gestures, you may also note that various qualities change the intention of the gesture. Being aware of how you use gestures can allow you to make definite choices, while respecting your listener. Perhaps you notice that you are making pushing gestures when in reality you are wanting to lift and support your listener. Having this physical awareness will allow you to choose a gesture and quality that will support your intention.

FIGURE 5.1 Two actors with arms up to two actors with open palms down. Photograph by Melis Derya White. Actors from L to R: Luis Alfonso Castro, Arleth Lopez, Aslan Longoria, Omar Moreno

5
RADIATING AND RECEIVING

"To radiate on the stage means to give, to send out. Its counterpart is to receive. True acting is a constant exchange of the two. There are no moments on the stage when an actor can allow himself – or rather his character – to remain passive in this sense, without running the risk of weakening the audience's attention and creating the sensation of a psychological vacuum".

Michael Chekhov, To the Actor,
*Routledge, revised, 2002, courtesy of the
Michael Chekhov Estate*

Having had the honor of working with Mala Powers, an accomplished actress who was personally coached by Michael Chekhov and was the executor of his estate, I was privy to many details that Chekhov shared with her. One primary question that Michael Chekhov would ask Mala when he was coaching her on a role, was whether her character was predominantly radiating or receiving. You may relate this to whether a character is an extrovert or an introvert, but instead this refers to how the character works with energy. Do they send energy out to others around them, or do they draw energy in toward them? Neither is positive or negative, but instead further choices will determine how the radiating or receiving is delivered by a certain character. A character may be radiating goodwill toward all around them or radiating their disdain for all of life. A character may be receiving with curiosity and caring for others or receiving to use that information to manipulate. While in life we want to have a balance of both giving and receiving energy, contributing to and absorbing communication, characters are much more interesting when they are out of balance.

Exercise 1: Radiate and send your energy

If you can be standing in front of a window to see beyond the space you are in, that's ideal…or if you have a comfortable space outdoors, that works too. Otherwise, your imagination will lead you in this exercise. This Michael Chekhov exercise was originally taught to me by one of his protégé's, Blair Cutting, at the Michael Chekhov Studio in New York City. Having been in a very "method" class, where I did not relate well to the material, this work was amazingly freeing and I realized that I had experienced some of the technique as an 18-year-old actor while training at the National Shakespeare Conservatory in New York with our stage movement teacher, Peter Lobdell. This experience upholds the adage that if you aren't relating to one class find another, and eventually you will find your niche. NMCA President Lisa Dalton and I teach the sequence of this differently, but as has been said previously, there is no right or wrong, so find what you relate to best. You may find other teachers that have their own variations. I will give specific instructions with foot positions and directions but modify these to best suit your own uniqueness.

As you stand in the space, be in what is sometimes called a neutral stance, though as previously stated, I prefer to call it a universal stance as none of us are truly neutral – and thankfully so! For this stance, stand in the position where you feel balanced and grounded, your spine elongated, arms loose at your sides, eyes facing forward. I appreciate the Oxford Dictionary definition of universal: "existing everywhere or involving everyone". This represents the idea that incorporates your individual posture as you are part of everyone, and your unique energy is part of what exists everywhere. Acknowledging that your balanced stance is part of everyone and everything, take a few breaths in this position to feel calm and grounded. As you move through this exercise, inhale when you are in your universal, balanced stance, and exhale on the action, then sustain the energy. The following instructions provide defined footwork, but left and right could alternate depending on what feels right for you. Begin by stepping forward with your right foot, keeping the torso upright, and extending the arms forward, palms facing the earth. Employ your imagination to feel as if you are sending energy forward through every cell of your body…radiating energy through your fingertips, your eyes, your kneecaps. Hold and experience this energy being transmitted for a few moments, then return to your universal stance. Now step to the right with that right foot and arms extending out to the right. Once again imagine sending energy from every cell in this direction. Energy emanates from the forehead, the torso, the toes. After engaging your imagination to feel this energy, return to your universal stance. Now step out to the left, once again extending your arms, palms facing down, and fingers extended outwards. Radiate your energy in this direction, then return to your universal stance. Next step backward with your left foot, keeping the torso upright, and sending your open palms to face the space behind you. Send the energy behind you, increasing your awareness of that unseen space. Return to your universal stance. Next take just a slight step forward with the right foot and now point your fingertips down to the ground, as if you are sending energy into the earth knowing it will support you. Return to universal. Next bring your left foot slightly forward and reach your arms up to the sky, fingertips extended. Imagine sending that energy skyward as far as you can imagine, penetrating through the ceiling if you are indoors or if outside reaching beyond the blueness of the sky out into the universe.

Once you have completed this sequence of front, sides, back, down and up several times, freeze in the final position with the arms extended. With the eyes closed, slowly lower the arms down, bring your foot back underneath you, eventually letting the arms land at your sides. Be aware of the energy that you have radiated all around you – front, sides, back below, and above. This bubble of energy can be referenced as your kinesphere and once you are aware of it you can fill it with whatever is needed for any character you may portray – or simply with positive energy to carry you through a challenging life situation – or to bring your very best into an audition room.

If there were only one exercise I could retain from the techniques of Michael Chekhov, this would be it. Not only has this helped calm nerves when done as a preparation prior to an audition or interview, but it has helped me generate positive, optimistic energy when I have had to enter what I realize will be a tough life situation.

In the past I assigned this to students in a class, where they needed to do several rounds of this exercise, prior to any challenge they may face, with the intention to have a more positive outcome.

Many stories bore out the fact that this exercise did indeed allow participants to achieve a more positive outcome than expected in a life situation.

One compelling story was from Julie, a mother of five children, who always dreaded going to the grocery store. She reported that she performed this radiating exercise prior to going to the store, filling her kinesphere with positive energy. Julie reported that this trip to the store was unlike any before. The colors of the produce appeared vivid and beautiful. Previously she had never had conversations in the grocery store, but on this day other customers were asking what she thought of different products. As a result of making a choice on how to enter a situation and choosing to radiate positivity, her experience was changed.

Another situation that a participant reported was a time when she and her spouse were in an argument. Ellen asked her husband if they could take a break and come back in a bit to continue the discussion. Ellen then went to another room and went through the radiating exercise, filling her kinesphere with openness and understanding. Ellen reported that it made all the difference when she returned to the discussion with her husband, and they calmly reached a compromise together.

Exercise 2: Receive the energy

This same exercise can be utilized in a slightly different way, allowing you to become more receptive as may be needed for a receiving type character. Using the same structure, beginning in a universal stance, once again take a slight step forward with the right foot and extend the hands out in front of you. This time, rather than extending through the fingertips in one long line from your shoulder, try flexing your hands, so that your arms are outstretched from your shoulders, palms are facing out, you've bent at the wrists, and your fingertips now point upwards. Imagine that you are receiving energy through the palms and that the energy you are receiving travels throughout your entire body. Retract the hands keeping the palms open in a receiving mode as you return to your universal stance. Now step out to the right with your hands flexed and palms extending, imaging receiving the limitless energy that exists all around you. Again, retract the hands slowly, keeping them flexed, receiving that energy into the body letting it ground you as your hands come back to your sides. Repeat to the left, then back to center. As you take a step to the back, flex your hands, and receive energy from behind you – from where you can't even see, but trusting energy is there. Slowly draw that energy back into yourself. Next is the slight step forward, and with your palms now open and facing the earth, imagine how that core of energy deep within the earth can bubble up to you. After returning to center, drawing the energy from below into the body, now it's time to lift the arms up to the sky with a slight step forward with the left foot. Flex your hands so that your palms are open to the sky, receiving energy from as far out into the universe as you can imagine. Slowly bend the elbows and bring that energy down into you as you bring the arms back to your sides, allowing your hand to relax and imagining your kinesphere is now charged with receptive energy. Imagine that you are a predominantly receiving character now, ready to absorb everything and everyone around you. As with previous exercises this is neither positively nor negatively charged, but instead you would make a decision based on the character you are playing. Is this character humble and truly interested in others and their endeavors, and that is the quality of their receiving? Is this character needy and jealous, and wants to absorb the energy from those around them in order that they may feel more fulfilled? Both of these are a way that you could interpret creating a receiving character, dependent upon your analysis of the text you're working with.

Improvisation 1: Stroll through the park

Individually assign ½ of your group as radiating characters and the other ½ as receiving characters. It's ideal if no one knows what anyone else is doing so in the follow-up discussion you can discover what was successful in portraying these character types. This could be quickly done by having participants in a circle but facing outwards and walking by and flashing to each a sign which reads either Radiate or Receive. Now all participants start to move randomly in the space and imagine they are out for a stroll in a park and open to making casual conversation. Hellos may be followed by comments on the weather or other random topics that are influenced by the radiating or receiving energy of the characters. Once everyone has had a chance to interact with most others in the group, the exercise is brought to a close. A discussion can follow this first round, or, have everyone switch to the opposite of what they were doing, radiating, or receiving, and go through the improvisation one more time. Although there will now be an awareness of who is radiating and who is receiving, it allows everyone to experience both ways of working with energy, and if done following the discussion, everyone can incorporate feedback to be more effective with their radiating or receiving.

Discussion/Reflection

Were you all aware of who was receiving and who was radiating? What elements did you observe from these two different states of energy? Were you more comfortable with one rather than the other? Did you see certain character traits emerge from others or from yourself because of your radiating or receiving? How and where have you observed these energies in life – from actors/performers you have observed?

Improvisation 2: Radiate the word

This improv allows participants to be more specific about what they are radiating and allows receivers to take in whatever comes their way – remaining open. Two lines are formed so that each person is facing a partner. One line will be radiating, and the opposite line will be receiving. The radiators are shown a word and without any gestures, they simply look at their partner and radiate that quality toward them. As this is quite subtle, the results will vary, but this is an excellent way to have a performer internalize and communicate just via the eyes and the energy being exuded. This is excellent training for on-camera acting and the close-ups where a feeling must be seen without any movement. Once the radiating side has worked to communicate what they were given, teams then discuss what they received and then open it to the entire group, and the word/image is revealed. Oftentimes the exact word may not have been received, but a feeling similar to the connotation of that word has been. Some of the most potent acting can happen in silence, and you want to have the ability to radiate and receive whatever occurs in any moment.

Suggestions of images/feelings to radiate (and of course, come up with your own ideas – it's limitless!): Fear, Envy, Acceptance, Disgust, Admiration, Disappointment, Unconditional Love, Hatred, Remorse, Sadness, Glee, Awe, Curiosity, Rage.

Improvisation 3: Psychic connection

Try this same exercise, with one participant radiating a quality and the other receiving, but now they are back-to-back. If participants are comfortable, they could sit back-to-back, with their backs touching so there is a connection. Of course, this will be very challenging, but it can also prove to be quite energizing if even when back-to-back someone can pick up on the type of energy another is radiating to them. This also allows participants to keenly focus as they attempt to determine what a partner is sending them without any visual cues.

Discussion/Reflection

Were you successful in psychically feeling what your partner was sending? Even if not, did it allow you to increase your focus on your partner and experience energy that might be present?

Improvisation 4: Radiate and receive with qualities

This improv can be done simultaneously in pairs spread across a space or could be done with one team at a time in front of the others who become the audience. Slips of paper with radiating or receiving with qualities attached are given out randomly to everyone, without letting their partner know or the audience know if they are viewing. The images and feelings used previously can be used, but now receivers also have a quality to color the way they receive.

Suggestions for images/feelings to pair with radiating and receiving:

Radiate Glee	Receive with humility
Radiate Rage	Receive with understanding
Radiate Joy	Receive with reticence
Radiate Sadness	Receive with glee
Radiate Romantic Interest	Receive with grace
Radiate Distrust	Receive with absolute trust
Radiate Insecurity	Receive with confidence

Once radiating or receiving characters with qualities have been chosen, teams are put into scenarios. If teams are all active throughout the space, one scenario could be given for all. If teams are presenting to an audience, the scenario could repeat, or a new scenario could be given each time.

Ideas for scenarios:

- Co-workers creating an ad campaign for their boss
- Co-workers planning a surprise birthday party for their boss
- Co-workers figuring out a way to get out of work
- Co-workers trying to determine how to get a raise
- Siblings planning their parents' anniversary event
- Siblings in their parents' house explaining what they want when parents are gone
- Siblings discussing who is the favorite child
- Roommates determining where furniture should be placed
- Roommates deciding how to divide up the bills

Discussion/Reflection

What sort of energy did you get from your partner? Can you find an adjective for that energy? Did you feel your partner was radiating or receiving? How did their behavior affect you? Do you feel like these could be realistic portrayals? How might you replay the scene to further incorporate the prompts you were given and make it even stronger?

Improvisation 5: Angel walk (strengthen the ensemble)

This exercise has a focus on radiating and receiving but also on atmosphere so it could be presented after those exercises are done. Over many years this has proven to be a very powerful exercise for building connections within the group and personally uplifting each participant. It can be quite emotional for some, so prior to deciding to use this exercise you'd want to be certain it is appropriate for your particular group.

Prior to the event, the exercise is explained to the group. They will enter a particular atmosphere, form two lines facing each other, and then one at time will walk in the middle of the line with their eyes closed, in a receiving mode of energy. All the participants in the line will then radiate supportive energy to whomever is walking in the middle, being sure to keep them safe and give gentle nudges as necessary to keep them in the line. Consent must be given by all participants for this touching, prior to the event, and acceptance given if a participant is uncomfortable in participating. Other variations that involve no touch at all will be given after this first version. As the walker passes by through the line, those on the edges, radiating, may choose to accompany their radiation with a word or sentence of support such as "you are an amazing artist" or anything positive they may have witnessed during the work with the individual.

The leader will set up a space as a surprise for the participants, creating a warm and magical atmosphere. This can be accomplished by stringing holiday lights, using LED candles, star projectors, and/or other items that allow for a warm and inviting space. Gentle music should be incorporated into this space to further enhance the atmosphere. Once ready, the participants are blindfolded, or simply agree to keep their eyes closed, and form a chain holding hands. The leader, with perhaps helpers along the chain, safely guides the participants to this special place and upon entering, quietly instructs them to remove their blindfolds or open their eyes. Participants take in the atmosphere of the space and form two even lines facing each other. The leader then gently pulls out one participant, and they close their eyes and then slowly walk down the line of their peers. Again, consent for this gentle touching of the shoulders must be given prior to this exercise. They want to be in full receiving mode, so that they are accepting and appreciating all the supportive energy being sent. As the directions above described, those in the line now radiate supportive energy to the walker and may perhaps lean in to give some words of support though that is not a requirement. If there are two leaders, one may remain at the opposite end of the line to "catch" the walker once they have completed their journey, and to guide them back in line to become a radiating participant. If there is only one leader, they could calmly go to the end of the line to "catch" the first walker, and then ask them to "catch" the next walker while they return to the beginning of the line to start the next walker on their journey. Once each walker has completed their journey, they will be at the end of the line to become the next "catcher" and be sure their peer is safely and calmly returned to the line.

After everyone has had a turn walking and receiving the supportive energy of their peers, all once again hold hands and form a human chain to exit the space silently and return to wherever the journey began. This may be done at the end of a session as a conclusion, with little discussion, or as needed, group members may share how they felt during the exercise. Again, this can be quite personal and emotional depending on the group, and the leader needs to take care of the participants.

Version 2

This was quite effective during the height of the pandemic when touch was not an option and space between all was necessary. For this version, the same magical space is set up with lights and music to create a warm and inviting atmosphere. Rather than holding hands and making a chain, everyone can retain their distance and simply walk to the magical space, which should surprise them with the atmosphere that's been created. Everyone then sits in the space at a distance that makes them comfortable. Everyone will have slips of paper and a writing utensil available in the space for their use, as well as a container of some sort. Glass vases which are readily and inexpensively available could be the containers for the exercise and contribute to the grace of the space. Now one person at a time will venture to the front of the space in a chair that has been set up, perhaps even a high stool, with their container. They now enter a receiving mode and can choose to have their eyes open or closed. A table by the chair can provide a resting space for their container. The rest of the participants now radiate support and good will to their peer at the front of the room. As inspired, peers now can write a word, phrase, or sentence on their slip of paper and then walk to the front and drop it into the container. This may be as simple as "amazing performer" or "grateful for you" or whatever positive word/phrase may come to mind. It may be that some peers will not write but simply choose to radiate the support and good will. Once the person in front senses that everyone wanting to contribute to the container has done so they take their container and return to their seat. A leader may be observing and calmly say "thank you" to cue the person in front to return, particularly necessary if the receiver chooses to have their eyes closed as they receive the radiant support from their peers. This continues until everyone has had a chance to be in the front and receive energy and perhaps slips of paper from their peers. The group then silently exits the atmosphere and returns to where the journey started and concludes with whatever discussion may be warranted – or simply exit with their containers of good will. In the past, participants have expressed being quite happy with the fact that they had these bits of paper that supported and uplifted them with radiant words.

Version 3

If you have access to an open, comfortable, and private outdoor space, then here's another version which combines connection while still refraining from touch. For this you use long pool noodles to connect everyone together. This way participants can still close their eyes and/or wear blindfolds, if the train of people can be safely led to the magical outdoor space that can be created. Battery powered LED lights can be used if there's not an outlet nearby, and a phone with a speaker for sound. The leader will bring the participants to the atmospheric outside space, and the darkness of night with magical lights shining is an especially effective time for this exercise. Participants circle up in the outdoor space, sitting on blankets or chairs that are provided. One participant at a time then enters the center of the circle and opens to receive the supportive energy from their peers, who are radiating all around. They may choose to stand, thereby having the ability to move around to see all in the circle or be seated, or the group can form a semi-circle so everyone can be seen at once. If you know your group appreciates technology, the positive affirmations for whomever is receiving can be radiated via text messages – just being sure everyone has everyone else's phone number. Otherwise, similarly to the last version, each person can have a container while others have paper and writing utensils and if they choose, they will write and drop their paper into the receiver's container. Once everyone has had a chance to be a receiver, the group rises and once again grabs the ends of the pool noodles and forms a chain to return to the starting point.

Improvisation 6: Nurtured by nature (contributed by Susan Schuld, Professional Vocal Coach, Professor at the University of Florida, and Certified Teacher via NMCA)

Imagine you are a seed buried in the earth, surrounded by cool, moist soil.

As you drink in the nutrients from the soil, experience the sensation of receiving.

Begin to germinate, sprout, grow. As you are expanding with each breath, experience the sensation of radiating.

Push through the earth as you grow into the sunlight and continue to experience the sensation of radiating.

As your roots drink in more moisture, experience the sensation of receiving.

Stand tall in your full growth and radiate into the warm sun that is pouring over your body.

Clouds drift overhead and it becomes cool and pleasant.

It begins to rain softly and receive the water trickling down your stems, petals, branches, and leaves.

The sun peeks out through the clouds, and you radiate up into the rainbow that has appeared.

Wrap up

Improvise to radiate and receive energy as a solo exercise, and then interacting with a group. Determine the differences between these two distinct ways of being and how characters may be predominantly one or the other. The dialogue can be simply about the weather or location, allowing the radiating or receiving energy to guide the conversation. Lines can face each other and work to now radiate specific qualities, and then check with partners as to what was received. Scenarios can be created with duos pursuing objectives but working as either a radiating or receiving character. As an ensemble builder for a willing group, the angel walk can allow everyone to radiate and receive as an artist, thereby building connection and individual confidence.

Solo application

While working on your own experiment with radiating your energy outward or being open to receiving energy and how each one feels to you. Observe when you naturally fall into one of these two energy patterns.

Script application

As Michael Chekhov asked Mala Powers, ask yourself if your character is predominantly radiating or receiving and acknowledge when in the script that may alter. Allow your character's energy to help determine how you will play a scene. You may also note qualities, such as radiating with benevolence or receiving with disdain. As with the other techniques, neither is positive or negative but instead your character and the action will dictate the way energy is radiated or received. In examining your text, you may realize that a character may switch from radiating to receiving, depending upon the situation. Employing these energetic changes can add subtlety and nuance to a performance.

Life application

The stories relayed above give testimony to how mastering this technique can greatly benefit you in life. Being able to manifest radiant energy when you are in need of it, such as for a presentation or simply to be present in a life situation is a valuable skill. To put yourself into a receiving mode can allow you to become a more compassionate listener and to let your ego relax and allow others to take center stage, giving them support and caring.

FIGURE 6.1 Three actors with one in back rising and one forward falling. Photograph by Melis Derya White. Actors L to R: Arleth Lopez, Aslan Longoria, Omar Moreno

6

THE THREE SISTER SENSATIONS

BALANCING, FALLING, FLOATING

"In the three-dimensional world, any object can be identified either as Falling, Floating, or Balancing. This includes our bodies, our breath, and our eyes. Likewise, intangible energies such as our thoughts, feelings, desires, spirit, centers, and personal atmospheres have their own degree of stability and can be described with these three sensations".
Lisa Dalton (President and Co-Founder of NMCA), Address at the International Michael Chekhov Symposium 2007, Sorbonne

Introduced after Michael Chekhov had passed, NMCA President Lisa Dalton brought these forth under the direction of Jack Colvin, a protégé of Michael Chekhov's, in the UK at an international conference. Originally Jack introduced floating as rising, but eventually changed it to floating, realizing that rising had the connotation of an upward movement but that a float had more possibilities as it could go in any direction. This chapter guides you to experience these states of equilibrium which we are all familiar with in life – struggling for balance when all around you may be a bit chaotic; falling whether it is with despair or relief; and floating which may reflect buoyant happiness or an urge to escape. The boundless interpretation of any of these techniques is a true testimony to Michael Chekhov's creative imagination and allows for you to determine how you will utilize any of these tools for your character or in your life.

Exercise: Experience the sensations – known as the Three Sisters

You may experiment on your own with these sensations, or if working with a group each individual can find their own area in the space in which to work. First explore the sensations of falling, being sure with all these sensations to remain conscious of your movement in order to stay safe. In a classroom an instructor may be able to utilize thick mats for safety, or practicing at home falling on a soft bed can allow one to experience the sensation. If you are agile and feel comfortable, you might literally fall (safely!) to the ground. Once you are on the ground, can you work with the sensation of falling up? One example of falling up that may have happened to many of us is falling up some stairs. The idea is to experience a sensation of falling and therefore that fall can go in any direction, not just down but to the back, sideways, and up. Be aware of what you are feeling as you are falling. This is once again a psycho-physical exercise, in that the physical motion can create a connection to your psychology and create feeling. Work with all parts of your body. You can let a finger fall, the hand fall, or your entire arm fall. Your eyelids can fall. Your head can fall. A knee could fall to the side and your heel might fall to the back. Work not only with your entire self falling, but with all these individual parts of you as they will then create their own micro-sensations of falling and affect you in unique ways. Be aware of what happens with your breath, and as you fall, let sound come out on your exhalation. As always, surprise yourself with this sound and however it manifests is perfect. Once you have taken time to experience the sensation of falling in all directions, simply walk through the space, upright, but now using just your imagination, with the physical expression veiled, continue to experience the sensation of falling. Be aware of how you are feeling as you move with this sensation of falling, and how you are seeing the world around you. Returning to your individual space, begin to move again but now allow all your movements to have a sensation of floating. Again, be sure to experiment with floating in all directions. You may feel that floating has an upward motion, but know that you can float down, just as a feather may gradually descend from the sky to the earth, or you can float to the side as that same feather may do in response to a gentle breeze. Be open to what you are feeling as you physically move with the sensation of floating in all directions. Be sure to float with various parts of the body, in addition to your body as a whole. Let your nose begin to float in all directions, or your elbow float and lead you through the space. This exploration can be endless as all parts of you experience floating in a multitude of directions. Be aware of your breath and let sound escape as you float so you become comfortable with how floating affects your voice. Next, veil the physical expression of the float and just walk through the space, but keeping the sensation of floating within you. Be aware of how this float affects your overall walk and how you are looking out at the world around you. Next, you'll work on the sensation of balancing. More accurately you want to experience the struggle for balance. While in life, humans typically strive to live in balance as much as they can and even our expressions bear out that pursuit: Balancing our budget, finding work-life balance, balancing our relationships, or balancing the chores within your household group. While as humans finding balance can lead to a sensation of calmness and control, characters are often out of balance and struggling to find balance. For this physical exploration, you want to experience that struggle for balance. One simple way to do this is lifting one foot off the floor, and then rising onto the ball of the other foot. Pretty quickly you will experience how your body is struggling for balance. As always, be conscious of your own physical limits, knowing that you can quickly return your foot to the floor and not fall! This could also be done on thick mats as mentioned above if available so that if someone truly goes into falling from this struggle for balance, they will have a soft and safe landing. You may also choose to keep both feet on the floor, but if you cross your legs while standing, with your feet next to each other but now on opposite sides of where they usually are, then lift your heels, you will also experience that sensation of struggling for balance. Another word to use that may help with finding this sensation is teetering. Imagine the tightrope walker who is struggling for balance putting one foot in front of the other on the highwire. You could try this, stepping one foot out directly in front of the other in a straight line, but then lifting your heels as you start to walk forward. The image of an officer asking someone who they believe is inebriated to walk a straight line may come to mind – you can imagine how that person is struggling for balance in that moment! This sensation can create a challenge for the breath and voice so be sure to fully explore what is happening for you. The breath may be held for a moment, and then may have a strong release as you recover for an instant and then perhaps a deep and sudden inhalation as you struggle again to balance. Allow sound to come out during the balancing and it will most likely be very erratic and full of range if you truly let it simply respond to the sensation. As a leader you may need to model and coach everyone to let go of vocal control during this struggle for balance and instead to just let the sound escape and be whatever it will be.

Discussion/Reflection

What feelings arose within you from these sensations? What happened as different parts of the body experienced the sensations – did different feelings or even character ideas come to light for you? What occurred as you walked with the sensations veiled? Did each sensation have its own tempo and did any have a distinct rhythm for you? Did you see the world around you in a different way depending upon which sensation you were working with?

Improvisation 1: Veiled greetings

Everyone will once again begin in their own space and move once again with a sensation of falling. Once they have gained that sensation, they move around the space as they did individually with the physical expression veiled. The leader will now ask them to be aware of their breath. How does the sensation of falling affect their breathing? Does the breath fall in more deeply? Does the breath seem to fall out of them too quickly so that the breathing has become shallower? Everyone now allows a bit of sound to come out as they are exhaling to discover the vocal tone that comes from the sensation of falling. Once that tone is discovered, everyone is now encouraged to greet everyone else in the space, maintaining the sensation of falling. Once everyone has had some time to interact, they return to their individual space and move on to floating and balancing and with each bring these sensations into the space and greet everyone they contact. Next the leader could assign one third of the group to fall, another third to float, and the other third to balance. Once again everyone works individually to be sure these sensations are active and then walk. Now the greetings will be an interesting mixture of "characters" and everyone can observe how they felt when approached by someone experiencing a completely different sensation.

Discussion/Reflection

How did you feel interacting with each of the sensations? Was there a certain type of energy that pervaded the room with each of the sensations? How did you feel when others were in a very different sensation than you? Did you feel influenced by their sensation and wanted to join them in their sensation, or did you feel your sensation was more dominant? Could you imagine that in playing a scene you might change in response to another character bringing in their own sensations?

Improvisation 2: Mirror with a twist

The group will divide in half, and make two concentric circles, with the group on the inside facing someone on the outside. Now begins the classic theatre mirror exercise. Whomever is on the outside of the circle begins a movement and the partner facing them from the inside circle mirrors that movement. A reminder that it is a mirror so it means if the outside player moves their left arm the inside player will be moving their right arm. Leaders should be sure to do movements that the other person can follow – you are not trying to challenge them but instead work in harmony with them, so you are moving in unison. You should also keep eye contact the entire time, using your peripheral vision to see what's happening with your partner rather than glancing away. This way you keep a strong connection. Once this connection is established and the mirrored movement is underway, the leader calls out "Falling movements!" and the leader now allows all their movements to embody a falling quality. The leader side coaches that the falling can happen in any direction – you can fall to the side and even fall up. After a time, the leader will call, "Switch! Inside take over as leader from right where you are – continue with falling movements". The inside person is now the leader of the movement. After a while, the leader will call "Freeze and drop!" and everyone stops and lets go of whatever position they are in. The leader instructs the inner circle only to move one person to their right. You now have a brand-new partner. Take a moment to establish eye contact and this time the inner person is instructed to begin general movement to establish this team's connection. Once the connection is established, the leader will call out, "Now all movements have a balancing quality to them!" The inner person will now let all their movements have a sensation of balance to them, still being sure that their partner who is mirroring them can follow. After a time, the outside person is instructed to take over the balancing movements from wherever the inner person left off. After a time, the leader will once again call "Freeze and drop!" and the connection ends and everyone lets go of their last positions. Once again, the leader will instruct the inner circle only to move one person to their right and to greet their new partner and establish eye contact. This time the outer person begins the general movement and after a time the leader will call out, "Floating movements!" Now all the movements contain the sensation of floating and can be in any direction – floating down toward the earth, up to the sky, or out to the sides. After a time, the leader will call out for everyone from the inner circle to take over and continue to float. This improvised movement with the three sister sensations can be repeated until everyone in the inner circle has been able to pair with someone in the outer circle.

Discussion/Reflection

Were you able to follow your partner? Did you enjoy leading or following more and why? As the leader, did you take care of your partner, being sure that they could indeed follow? How was it different with different partners? Did you sense different energy from each individual? Did everyone have different versions of these sensations and as the mirror were you able to experience them in different ways? What happened as you moved with the three sister sensations? How did the movement change? Did any feelings come up that you associated with these movements?

Improvisation 3: What's happening with the weather?

For this improv, everyone is divided into teams of two and one team of three if there's an odd number. Everyone is then assigned a characteristic based upon one of the Three Sister sensations. This could be assigned from drawing slips of paper or dividing up each team into A's and B's and maybe a C, and then having them look over to the leader who holds up a sign for all the A's, all the B's and the C's, while others have their backs turned. Rather than simply interacting with the sensations, now what is probably a familiar term linked to a sensation will be the impulse used. The topic should be the weather and teams should work to stay within that topic, though they might go off on a tangent due to organically responding to their partner(s). Once everyone is amid their chats about the weather, the leader can call freeze and let everyone know to stay concentrating, but to now focus on one scene that the leader asks to "unfreeze". This allows for each team to now have an audience and for everyone to enjoy what is happening with different manifestations of each sensation.

The expressions that can associate with each sensation can be created by the ensemble and then utilized by the leader, or the leader can provide them. It's fun to create your own ideas and to discover the expressions from life associated with these sensations, and here are some to get the improvisation started.

A: Falling in Love
A: Balancing to find control
A: Floating in a sea of sadness
A: Falling apart
A: Balancing their fear
A: Floating with swelled head

B: Floating into space
B: Falling for an old trick
B: Balancing to find confidence
B: Floating in bliss
B: Falling in disgrace
B: Balancing their attraction

Discussion/Reflection

How did working with these sensations influence the way you communicated? What did you receive from others as a result of them employing a sensation?

Improvisation 4: Duo presentations

Provide a scenario for a duo to accomplish as characters. This could be planning a special party or practicing for a job interview – a task with an objective. Now the duo plays this scene, but always should be in a state of falling, struggling for balance, or floating. The participants can randomly choose one state to be in as they interact on how to achieve their objective. Another version is to instruct them that they can never be in the same state at the same time. At first, it's helpful to do these full-out, physically expressed, so that these sensations are truly experienced. Once they feel more ingrained, they can then be "veiled", so that the internal energy is still as strong, but the outward manifestation can be quite minimal. This version can result in complex subtext coming through via the voice and the subtler physicality that is realistic.

"Callers"

This technique can be used with many of the exercises when a duo is in front of an audience presenting. For this improv, the leader will ask for two volunteers, one for each of the two people up in front presenting. It is then established who will be the "caller" for whom. Then each caller gives their actor one of the three sister sensations with which they will start the scene. The scene begins, and at any point, the caller will call out a new sensation and the actor must immediately switch, while still maintaining the same dialogue and same situation.

Improvisation 5: Object plays (contributed by Nichole Hamilton, Professional Actor, theatre professor at New Mexico State University and Certified Teacher via NMCA)

Object play 1

Choose an object. Your object need not be special, just unbreakable. Perhaps a small pillow, a tissue, a pencil, a t-shirt, etc. With an awareness of gravity, begin to play with the object using the sensation of floating. Moving the object away from the earth and the force of gravitational pull, how does it feel for the object to float? Are there shifts in your breath and body while you play with the floating of the object? Play with the tempo of the object floating, how does your inner life perceive this sensation? Play with using the object floating above in various directions. Can the object rotate as it floats? Avoid the impulse for falling or balancing for now, and just play with the sensation of floating. When you are ready, pause the object in mid-float and then allow it to fall to the earth. This simple action of the object yielding to the gravitational pull can bring more awareness to the sensation of falling. When you are ready, float the object up again and then play with conscious control of the object falling. Play with tempo, direction, and invite the interplay of your breath and body into the sensation of falling. After exploring the object fully in falling, and before inviting the object to float again, what would happen if you could not pick up the object? Imagine attempting to float the object but gravity is pulling the object to the ground. Invite this physical struggle and tension in the sensation of balance. When ready, succeed in retrieving the item and return it to floating. Now explore balance in the other direction. Play with the object's intent to float but the gravitational pull is strong, but you must keep the object floating. What shifts do you sense in your breath and body? Continue to explore this sensation of balance in your own unique way. For discussion: When playing with the object in one of the three sensations, did a character situation present itself? Did an image spring into your mind? Did the object remain what it was in playing (literal) or did your imagination create a different prop (metaphorical)? From these seeds of inspiration, create your own improvisation, a story, or monologue, using the prop with the sensations of floating, falling, and balancing.

Object play 2

Playing Sensations within a Monologue. Use a familiar monologue. Play your monologue once rote (quickly, monotone, with no intent or subtext). Replay your monologue three times, each time using a different sensation unveiled for the value of play. After you have fully explored the monologue three times with curiosity in each unique sensation, use a sensation when there is a shift – a new character thought, a discovery, an emotional response, or a change in intent or tactic. Let the sensation play you. For discussion: Did you make any discoveries when using the sensation of floating, then with falling, then with balancing? Are there any sensations you might consciously choose to play in specific moments of the monologue? To what degree is it veiled or unveiled? Now replay your monologue, but consciously choose a sensation when there is a shift to aid in more specific crafting and allowing for your character's transitions while stirring you the actor's inner life.

Object play 3

Playing Sensations within a Scene. Invite a partner to play. Choose a familiar scene, one which you do not need to rely on the script. Each actor plays with one sensation fully throughout the scene. Use this without logic or reasoning. Play with each sensation fully, unveiled. Then replay the scene, inviting an authentic response to your partner, shifting sensations spontaneously when feeling a new beat, transition, or response. This may be unveiled or veiled.

If you do not have a familiar scene, an open scene is provided below. There are no given circumstances, subtext, or intent. With a partner, memorize the lines rote. When you feel shifts, changes of beats, play spontaneously with a sensation of floating, falling, or balancing. Begin playing the sensation in a fully unveiled way. Then play authentically with degrees of veiling or unveiling. For discussion: How did physical exploration of sensations stir the inner life? How did you affect your partner's response with a sensation? How were your responses affected by your partner's use of sensation? Now replay your scene, but consciously choose a sensation when there is a shift to aid in more specific crafting and allowing for your character's transitions while stirring you the actor's inner life.

Open Scene A: Are you ready? B: No A: Why not? B: I don't know A: What's wrong with you? B: I don't know A: Are you in love? B: Maybe A: Oh no B: Don't say that A: I can't help it B: Why are you always like this?

Wrap up

Work solo to experience these three sister sensations and be aware of how they manifest in everyday life. Mingle and improvise greetings and simple conversations to get more familiar with the sensations and how they manifest for you, in body and voice. Try a mirror circle to experience the way others interpret falling, balancing, and floating. Try a simple group improv talking about the weather while experiencing these sensations. Work up to a duo improvised scene with an objective, randomly changing sensations or employing callers to surprise you with the changes.

Solo application

Continue to physically explore the variety of ways you can experience falling, floating, and struggling for balance. What happens when your gaze falls or floats? What if your hands feel out of balance and you struggle to calm them? Building the physical vocabulary of these three sister sensations will allow you more nuances when creating a role.

Script application

In analyzing a script, imagine when your character may be falling, struggling to maintain balance, or floating – and you can add qualities to these sensations to be more precise. You may be falling with sadness or falling in love; floating in bliss or floating in fear; struggling to balance unexpected joy or struggling to balance evil forces. Your analysis of your character and the story will lead your imagination to make choices. With these choices then noted in the margins of the script you will have specific sensations to try.

Life application

Empathy is a powerful mode of understanding and communication and being familiar with these sensations can help you be supportive of others that you may witness falling or struggling for balance. Perhaps you can recognize their floating and allow yourself to share that sensation of lightness. Being familiar with these will allow you to reflect on your own state of being, and, if wanted, make a choice to change it.

FIGURE 7.1 Actors exploring a column. Photograph by Melis Derya White. Actors L to R: Omar Moreno, Shawn Pirkle, Luis Alfonso Castro, Arleth Lopez, Aslan Longoria

7

QUALITIES AND SENSATIONS

> *"The individual feelings of an actor are, or might at any time become, very mercurial and capricious. You can't order yourself to feel truly sorry or gay, to love or to hate. Too often are actors compelled to pretend that they are feeling on the stage, too numerous their unsuccessful attempts to squeeze these feelings out of themselves… True artistic feelings, if they refuse to appear by themselves, must be coaxed by some technical means which will make an actor the master over them".*
>
> Michael Chekhov, To the Actor,
> Routledge, revised, 2002, courtesy of the
> Michael Chekhov Estate

This chapter introduces you to one of Michael Chekhov's alternatives to using your own personal experiences to reveal the feelings of a character. The concept is that we have all experienced and/or observed a plethora of feelings, and rather than needing to conjure up a personal memory that could be harmful to us psychologically, we can instead use our muscle memory to move with a certain quality and allow that movement to infuse us with sensation which may then lead to feeling. For an actor, the shocking revelation may be that you don't have to have the feeling, but that instead as a storyteller you convey the feeling so that the audience can have the experience. While in some circles this may be a controversial assertion, by improvising with various qualities you may very well realize the effectiveness of these techniques.

If you are not familiar with emotional recall, it's when an actor goes into their memories and searches for a time when they personally experienced an emotion that is called for in a current performance. The actor then recalls all the sensations involved via their five senses — what they were touching and what was touching them, any tastes, smells, what they were hearing in the moment and what they were seeing. By bringing back all these sensations, the expectation is that the emotion will then arise, and could be used in a current scene as needed. You may recall stories of actors using this technique, often associated with "Method" acting, and then not being able to let go of the emotion or the character they create. Conjuring up painful memories from the past can be psychologically damaging for some, and Michael Chekhov's techniques, for me, provide a healthier alternative. This is not to disparage other techniques, as many amazing actors certainly utilize emotion recall to great success and create stellar performances, but this is another way that emotions can be accessed to create those stellar performances.

This technique promotes a performer expanding their imagination and does not require tapping into personal events. Michael Chekhov witnessed, and you may have too, actors having difficulty with emotional recall which led to his exploration of other techniques toward a similar aim. In fact, there is a classic story about Michael Chekhov as a student in one of Constantin Stanislavski's classes, in which an exercise using a real-life event was to be presented. Michael Chekhov reenacted his father's funeral and was full of emotion and was praised in front of the class. However, later Stanislavski discovered that Michael Chekhov's father was indeed alive, and that Chekhov had made up the whole scene rather than drawing on a real-life experience. Chekhov was ousted from class and the records show Stanislavski listed it as due to an "overheated imagination".

Michael Chekhov and Stanislavski did mend ways, and Michael Chekhov became a premiere actor at the Moscow Art Theatre until he was forced to leave Russia to never return. There is also an account of Stella Adler, who was working with Lee Strasberg of the Actor's Studio in New York, visiting with Stanislavski in Paris. Adler was dismayed with the conjuring up of personal memories and emotions, and Stanislavski explained that it was just one small component to his method and suggested that Adler seek out Michael Chekhov. While Stella Adler returned to the U.S. and opened her own actor training studio which is thriving even now, upon her death Mala Powers did receive word that she had many boxes of notes on Michael Chekhov's work!

Exercise: Experience the variety of qualities

While we may not be able to force ourselves to have an emotion, what we can do is will ourselves to move with certain qualities. That is how this exercise begins, "moving with the quality of…", which may then lead to having an actual sensation and to a feeling bubbling through. Once this technique is exercised time and time again, it becomes quick and easy to access whatever emotion may be required for a performance. This exercise is an introduction, but you will want to repeat this many times to be facile with qualities becoming sensations to feelings, and while several are listed here, you should explore the myriad of emotions that you may be called upon to portray as a performer.

Either working solo or if in a group, maintaining your concentration on your own experience to begin, start to move with a quality of curiosity. Being curious is something everyone has typically experienced, or, as with any of these, has observed. The terrific thing about all these techniques is that if something isn't coming to you, then just pretend that it is. Isn't that what acting is – pretending? It is often with pretending that we will reach something solid to then use. Moving about the space with this quality of curiosity, start to look at everything around you with this quality. Perhaps moving with this quality inspires you to reach out to an object with open palms to feel its texture. Perhaps you look deeply into a corner of the space you are working in which you had not done before. Be aware if moving with this quality of curiosity, which you can command yourself to do, starts to produce the sensation of curiosity within you. You may feel a tingling sensation of curiosity in your limbs and then you may realize that you are feeling curious as you continue to explore the space. Once you've spent some time in curiosity, let that go, shake it away, and come back to your universal stance. Now begin to move with a quality of fear. You have surely experienced fear, whether via a haunted house, the sighting of a snake or spider, or even when watching a scary movie. Therefore, you already know how to move with the quality of fear and don't have to rely on remembering any of your own fearful moments. Instead, you are simply moving through space with the quality of fear. Look through the eyes of fear at the space and items around you. You will undoubtedly be seeing these in a very different way than through the eyes of curiosity. Continue to move through the space, with every part of your body moving with the quality of fear and note if you start to feel sensations of fear coursing through your body. Then you may even realize you are feeling fearful although you are in a space that is typically safe for you. This is the artist in you creating via your imagination – a key to successful performance. After spending a bit of time in fear, shake this out thoroughly – letting it completely go. Whenever you are working on exercises, particularly when they encompass strong emotion, you want to be sure and clear by ending with something that is more positive. For this third and final exploration, begin to move with a quality of joy. Find that quality in your fingers – how do they move with a quality of joy? Do those fingers start to dance, to flick, to fly through the air? Let all of your body parts move joyfully. This can get quite silly and so it should. Let your feet bounce or tap with joy. Allow that quality of joy to be in your knees, your elbows, your cheeks. You may then realize sensations of joy are streaming through the body and creating feelings of joy within you – even though you didn't have to focus on anything in particular – you are simply manifesting joy as a creative artist! As hard as it may be to let go of the joy, shake that out and return to your universal stance.

Depending upon time, many more qualities can be explored. This exercise can be repeated countless times so that participants become facile with various qualities of movements and can more quickly connect to the sensations that may arise and create feelings.

Other qualities with which you can move: Angrily, ragefully, tenderly, vivaciously, enviously, defeatedly, melancholically – keep discovering more!

Discussion/Reflection

Were you able to note sensations after moving with certain qualities? Did some come easier than others and if so which ones? Did feelings arise that felt quite real to you? Which ones? Can you identify why some may be easier for you than others? Can you imagine how moving with a quality can communicate what's needed in a story to an audience, even if you are not quite feeling it?

Improvisation 1: A journey through sensations

This journey will allow you to viscerally experience a variety of sensations that may just inspire certain feelings and provide you with a way for your imagination to link to a feeling. For this exercise, a leader will want to set up a variety of stations that contain items that can influence the senses. Prior to this activity, the leader wants to check with all participants regarding any allergies or sensations that may be triggering. Once this is known, there should be a variety of objects available that have different textures, such as a rock, a feather, and a piece of clay. You'll want there to be a variety of smells, which may range from cologne to vinegar. There should be items that can be tasted, representing a range, such as lemons to dark chocolate – again, being sure not to bring anything into the space which could cause a negative reaction from any individual. Noisemakers that can be heard might be whistles or harmonicas. The participants should not know what these items are, so they should be kept "under wraps" until the exercise is about to begin. You will also need blindfolds for this exercise. By removing the sense of sight which many of us rely on so heavily, the other senses will become more heightened. You will want to be aware of and sensitive to anyone in the group that has any sensorial impairments and adjust the exercise accordingly. The group will divide into teams of two, with one person of each team as the leader and the other will follow and will be blindfolded. The leader of the duo needs to check with their partner once again to discover if there are any allergies, or just a vehement dislike, whether that be to any food items or lotions, sensitivities to perfume, etc., so that they can care for their partner as the exercise proceeds. It is also advisable for the leader of each duo to have their partner's water bottle as a sip may be wanted after tasting certain items. The leader also wants to establish the comfort level of the partner in terms of touch…are they okay being led by holding their hand or is it better to gently guide a shoulder. If actual touch is not advisable, pool noodles could be used to guide the partner so that there can be distance and no actual touch is needed. One partner could hold one end of the noodle and be gently pulled along to each station containing the items to explore, and/or the pool noodle could be used as a gentle prod on the arm or hand as guidance to items. Once the guidelines are established, the follower secures their blindfold with the help of the partner if needed/requested, and the leader leads their blindfolded partner to one of the stations and hands them items, using only sound, no words, to guide them in exploring taste, touch, smell, sound, and feel. The leader or leaders can also contribute to these experiences by playing various sounds on a speaker system (if it is available) or on a cell phone, and traveling amidst the participants and/or using objects with texture to glide by the skin of participants – such as a (clean) feather duster? Once this team has advanced to several stations, then they return to the center of the room and switch places. Once again, the current leader ascertains from the follower their comfort level, obtains their water bottle, and the duo goes back out to the stations. Once this round is complete, the teams return to the center and blindfolds are removed and time is given to discuss the activity.

Discussion/Reflection

Did you always know what you were touching, smelling, hearing, or tasting? Did you experience a variety of sensations as a result of what you touched, tasted, heard, and smelled and what were they? Did these sensations bring about any feelings? Did you have strong reactions to certain sensations – positive or negative? Could you see how focusing on one of these sensations could be beneficial when creating a role?

Improvisation 2: Sensational characters

Now that everyone has experienced a variety of sensations, the group is asked to form a large circle, so that everyone has space around them, and to turn their backs to the circle. Now everyone is instructed to begin physicalizing their reactions to the various sensations. This then becomes another psycho-physical exercise where the sensation now begins to inform the psychology. Be sure to incorporate the entire body so if the sensation is from a sour lemon, let the whole body react to that sourness, from the head down to the toes. Continue to play with these sensations and realize you are building a repertoire of sensations and your own unique, individualized reactions to them. As with other exercises, you will want to continue this type of exploration so that you are then familiar with what sensations can provide you with a prompt that may lead to a feeling as needed for a certain character. Now, on to these characters! Imagine that one of the sensations you have been working with becomes the impulse for a character. Bringing back the lemon, perhaps your imagination brings to you a "sourpuss" character. With your back still turned to the outside of the circle, imagine how your chosen character would greet a group, based upon the sensation you choose. You may have experienced a sensation of shyness from a certain object and your physical expression may center around being contracted. Perhaps you experienced a joyous sensation, and a character is inspired to start jumping with both arms waving. As always, there is no right, or wrong to any of these artistic expressions. What does your character say as a greeting and how does this voice sound? Now that you have a greeting, complete with a gesture plus a word or phrase – or perhaps just a sound, add one more statement for this character to share. Fill in the blank: "My favorite thing is…". Let anything just come to you and practice that a few times – it may even morph as you practice it. When ready, turn to the center of the circle and then whenever anyone is ready, greet the group, and let them know your favorite thing, all inspired by the sensations you previously experienced. Once one person goes, continue the greetings around the circle to the right so everyone has a chance to greet and share their statement.

Discussion/Reflection

Were you comfortable improvising a greeting? How easily did something come to you? Did an impulse come to you quickly and easily based on one of your experiences during the exercise? Did something quickly fill in the blank to be your favorite thing? Did you feel successful in allowing a sensation to assist in the creation of this character? Do you feel you'd have a bevy of feelings and characters you could create based on the sensations you experienced?

Improvisation 3: Present!

For this improvisation a duo or trio is put in the performance space with several items that have their own quality or inspire a sensation. Ideally, the items for the blindfolded sensations walk are used for this, and placed on a large table. The basic scenario is that shop owners are deciding which of these items on the table to retain for their retail business, and which they should discontinue. For this improvisation, an item must be in the hands of each performer at all times and can be switched at random. The qualities of the item in hand and the sensations it inspires, must be incorporated into the scene. As an example, if one character is holding a lemon and interprets that item as sour, they may then begin behaving very sourly about every item in the store. Another character may be holding chocolate and be just as sweet as can be about everything being said. It will be from these perspectives that the characters will discuss whether to keep the lemon and/or the chocolate as items in the store. There is no negative or positive to any item, as the "sour" character may love that sensation and want to keep the lemon and the "sweet" character may also love the lemon in contrast to the chocolate – anything goes! At any time, a character will put down one item and pick up another, and the dialogue must continue where it left off, but now a new sensation will inform where that dialogue goes.

Discussion/Reflection

Did you feel that the items did bring you a specific quality or sensation? Did any feelings arise from working with that quality or sensation? Were you able to continue the dialogue even when you switched items and a new sensation occurred?

Improvisation 4 (contributed by Geoffrey Arndt, Theatre Director, Instructor at Chicago's Loyola Academy and Certified Teacher via NMCA)

"Tasks with qualities"

In this exercise, we will explore qualities and sensations through a series of everyday tasks, and how qualities added to a series of tasks awaken sensations that may not typically be associated with the task. Begin by choosing a task for yourself – if working without an instructor or group – or a task for the group to explore – if working with a group. Improvise this task through a sequence of movements that have a clear beginning, middle, and end. Suggestions could be washing dishes, tying your shoe, or folding a letter and placing it in an envelope. Once you have a sequence of movements, add specific qualities to your sequence. You could complete the task with a quality of "sadness", then repeat your sequence moving "angrily", a very different quality, or with a quality of "anticipation". Once you have explored your sequence with a few different qualities, create a longer sequence where you enter a room, complete two or three sequences of tasks, then exit. After creating this entrance and exit series of tasks, invite the group – if working with a group – to yell out different qualities while you perform this entrance and exit series of tasks. If working without an instructor or group, decide on a few different qualities that will change how you complete this series of tasks. Consider using polarity by choosing qualities that are opposite throughout your series of tasks.

Wrap up

While you can't force yourself to feel, you can make a choice to move with a certain quality, and let that quality also be in your voice. Explore moving with various qualities and allow the possibilities for sensations to arise that then lead to feelings. Explore items with all your senses to broaden your vocabulary of qualities and your reactions. Take these varied sensations into improvisation to discover character and feelings.

Solo application

Take time to plug into your senses during everyday experiences so that you can increase your awareness and be able to utilize varied qualities and sensations as a performer. On your own move and speak with a chosen quality and allow sensations and feelings to arise, knowing that your own will power allows you to make choices.

Script application

Being familiar with qualities and sensations will allow you to create a score in your script that can be very creative. Perhaps you see your character as quite sour in a section and you can note that, or perhaps writing lemon will cue you in to that sensation and feeling. From the more obvious qualities such as sadness or anger, to finding the more imaginative ways those may manifest for you via your imagination, you can write what will inspire you for your character's journey. You may write shredded ribbon next to a section of sadness if that inspires you or rusty nail next to a section of anger if that prompts those feelings in a particular way for your character. The exciting concept for qualities and sensations leading to feelings is that you don't have to pull up your personal emotions which can infringe upon your life when not performing and often are not reliable performance after performance. Your tool instead is your imagination which brings you vivid qualities to be applied.

Life application

Allowing yourself to be vulnerable and to experience a myriad of qualities and sensations will give you the ability to empathize with and more readily understand the experience of others. Being aware of how your imagination can bring a new quality/sensation to you and thereby alter your own feelings, can be quite handy when you want to get out of a certain mood or need to enter a situation that you don't feel in the mood for. Particularly if you feel entering a challenging situation is required, you can use your imagination to move with a certain quality, let the accompanying sensation arise, and then allow that sensation to govern your physicality, thereby changing your experience. Perhaps you are feeling nervous about an audition, but instead want to feel a calm readiness. Dig into your imagination to discover what has that quality of calm readiness for you? Perhaps you simply move in space with the quality of calmness until the sensation of calmness is in you. Perhaps an image, such as that of a vibrant green leaf being gently caressed by a breeze allows you to sense the calmness. Moving in that way might not only provide a sensation of peaceful calm but may add a sensation of flexibility via the breeze, leading to a wonderful combination of useful feelings. What a wonderful way to enter an audition – vibrant, calm, and flexible! Our imagination is a powerful tool and the more we work with it, the more facile we become.

FIGURE 8.1 Five actors in a line leading with varied parts of the body. Photograph by Melis Derya White. Actors L to R: Luis Alfonso Castro, Arleth Lopez, Aslan Longoria, Omar Moreno, Shawn Pirkle

8
MOVEABLE CENTERS

> *"The imaginary center in your chest will also give you the sensation that your whole body is approaching, as it were, an 'ideal' type of human body. Like a musician who can play only on a well-tuned instrument, so you will have the feeling that your 'ideal' body enables you to make the greatest possible use of it, to give it all kinds of characteristic features demanded by the part you are working on".*
>
> Michael Chekhov, To the Actor,
> Routledge, revised, 2002, courtesy of the
> Michael Chekhov estate

The concept of moveable centers is that by choosing a distinct place from which a character's energy emanates, you can quickly create a unique character. Each center will have a location, a quality or image, and a sense of movement – though perhaps the choice is that the center is not moving at all. You might also experiment with centers that are outside of you. Before experimenting with these centers, the first step is to create a "home base", a center where you can return to and drop any character created. This concept is integral to the health of the actor. We have all heard stories about actors who maintain their characters even during breaks in filming, and at times bring those characters home to their family. The idea behind the techniques in this book and the spine of Michael Chekhov's work is that you act via your imagination and can readily drop any character or emotion created. The hope is to foster creative artists who are also healthy artists and can be contributors not only in the field of performance but in daily life as well. Now on to creating a healthy 'home base' center that can be a touchstone after any other creation.

Exercise: The artistic center

This exercise allows participants to discover what Michael Chekhov called the "artistic center", sometimes referred to as the "ideal artistic center". When speaking of "ideal" it's important that participants are assured that this is not any specific ideal outside themselves to strive for, but instead will be their own personal ideal. This will be a state of being that is comfortable and confident for each individual. To initially find this, participants should ideally be in a circle. Participants are asked to close their eyes and informed that a statement will be given, and they will respond with the question, "Who, me?" When they respond, they will point to themselves in a natural, organic way. The goal is not to be uniquely creative right now, but instead to respond honestly. To begin, arms are relaxed at the sides and participants are in a universal posture. Now, with the eyes closed the leader, with great enthusiasm, states, "You just won a million dollars!" The participants quickly respond with "Who, me?" Additional ideas to elicit a similar response, dependent upon the unique participants that are involved include the leader calling out, "Who is a creative artist?" and the participants answering, "I am", or the leader calling out, "Who had the willpower to show up here today?" with participants answering, "I did" or the leader calling out, "Who wants to be the best creative artist they can be?" with participants responding with, "I do". You can gauge what to say according to your own particular group. You could also adapt this for young students, working within the construct of their world with the leader calling out something akin to, "Who's excited for recess today?" and the students answering, "I am!" With all the ideas presented here, group leaders can utilize their unique creativity in finding what works best for them and those they are working with. Once this exchange happens, participants are asked to freeze whatever gesture they made when pointing to themselves and to now open their eyes and look around the circle. Most of the time, the gestures will be toward the upper chest. If someone is pointing mid-air, ask them to follow that line of energy and often it will wind up in that same upper chest area. Of course, there will be some other areas that are revealed, but this has been done in other countries, with translators, and still the majority have found this spot in the upper chest. This center, which is just a couple inches below the collar bone, residing in the slight indentation you may feel above the pectoral muscles, was noted as the artistic center by Michael Chekhov. This center should allow you to feel very upright, grounded, confident, and ready for whatever may be required of you next.

Discussion/Reflection

Were you able to point to yourself without thinking about or determining where you were going? Did most of the group find they referred to an area in the upper chest? Remember there are no "wrongs", so if you pointed somewhere else, then simply work with this location of the upper chest to see what it may bring you.

Improvisation 1: Walking through space

Once this artistic center is established, individuals now move around the space focusing on this center. The center, by the very name, is not on the surface, but is imagined to be inside the body, a sphere of energy centered within the cavity of the upper chest. This center can radiate energy in all directions like a bright ball of sunshine. To begin, the leader instructs participants to lightly tap that spot they have discovered, or have been led to, to awaken that center within. The leader side coaches while participants randomly walk, instructing them: allow that tapping to awaken that ball of energy in the upper chest. Once you have established an awareness of that energy and you are imagining it there, drop your arm and simply walk through the space, leading with this artistic center. Imagine that this artistic center in the upper chest allows you to walk with an open and balanced posture, with confidence, feeling grounded and secure, ready for anything. Be aware of your breath and know that moving with this center allows you to breathe deeply and with ease, the breath naturally flowing in and out, adding to your sense of calm and security. Know that at any time you can return to this center, back to this place of feeling grounded and secure, simply by using your imagination to activate this ball of energy once again, this ideal artistic center that is currently leading you through space.

Discussion/Reflection

Did you feel a difference with this walk and your own typical way of moving in space? If so, what were the differences? Were you able to relate to feeling grounded and confident? Did you notice a change in the atmosphere of the room when everyone was moving in this way?

Improvisation 2: Altering your center

Continue walking through the space with your ideal artistic center in the upper chest, feeling confident and secure, your "best" self. Now, imagine that center, that ball of energy, drops down into the belly – that's the new location. Imagine that this center is made up of jelly – that's the quality or image of the center. Next, imagine this center to be jiggling – that's the movement which the center has. Allow yourself to walk through space with this new center leading you. Imagine that both your physical self and the persona of this new jelly belly character emanate from this jiggling jelly. For learning purposes, allow yourself to express this center right now with full physical commitment. Exaggerate this to your fullest extent, allowing the entire body to alter because of this new center. You may move with a very different pace than how you were moving with your personal ideal artistic center. Perhaps you find a rhythm to your movement, inspired by the jiggling motion. What happens to your arms? Are they swinging more than usual or jiggling by your sides? Has your posture changed? How about the way your feet are touching the ground? Now bring the focus to your breath. Is there a change in your breath? Does that jelly bring the breath deeper down to the belly or is your breath shallower? Does your breath imitate the jiggling movement at all? Now let a touch of sound escape as you exhale. Surprise yourself – don't predetermine how it will sound – just let it be. It may be higher or lower than your typical voice. Perhaps it will be breathy, or nasal. Let this new center determine your new voice! Let your voice now form a greeting that works for this character. Again, don't predetermine what it will be, but just let that greeting happen, practicing it for yourself. This could be a "hello" or a "hi" or a "hey" or a "what's up" – whatever comes to you via this center. Now that this character is established individually, it's time to move onto group improvisation.

Discussion/Reflection

Were you able to imagine moving from this new center? Were you able to incorporate the location, quality, and sense of movement? Did you feel that your entire body responded to this center? What were the changes you discovered? Did a character begin to emerge for you?

Improvisation 3: Interactions!

Continuing the above, with your jelly belly character, a leader will now instruct you to notice the other characters moving through the space. You now want to greet each character that you pass by with the greeting you established previously. Be sure to not only greet, but to also listen and take in the greetings that are given to you, thereby being a receiver. Change your path as needed so you can be sure to greet every other character that is walking in the space. Once everyone has greeted each other the leader will ask that everyone once again focus just on themselves in space, and then allow that jelly belly center to instantly disappear and to once again become aware of their ideal artistic center in the upper chest. Allow that artistic center to bring back the feeling of being grounded, present, secure, confident, and ready for anything. Allow the breath to return to your own personal rhythm and continue to breathe and move through the space with ease.

Discussion/Reflection

What were the differences between you as your ideal artist with the center in the upper chest and the jelly belly character you created? What differences happened in your breath and then your voice? Were you able to quickly let go of the character and get back to your "best" self by imagining the center coming back to the upper chest? How might you further indulge in the exercise for even more results?

Group improvisation 4: Endless character centers

Here are just a few more suggestions for centers to be explored. Once these are explored individually, they can then be taken into improvisations. Remembering that each center has a location, an image/quality, and a range of movement will allow you to make up endless combinations. Here are just a few:

Location	Image/quality	Movement
Both heels of the feet	Metal springs	Bouncing
Tip of the nose	Shiny light	Beaming
Right knee	Helium balloon	Floating
Left shoulder	Ice cube	Melting
All fingertips	Match heads	Burning

Group improvisation 5: Freeze and share!

This improv begins with changing from the artistic center to a new location with a quality/image and sense of movement. Once again, each participant finds their own version of a character once these are assigned, moving through the space and connecting with the breath. The voice of the character is discovered by vocalizing on the exhale and then once again a greeting is practiced. Next, working at first solo, the following open-ended statements are given to the participants by the leader. Participants simply allow an answer to fill in the blank and then repeat that for themselves to become comfortable with their character's voice and the information revealed. All of these are from your character's point of view. The first statement, "My name is…" and just let something organically pop in – trusting something will come. Once again, surprise yourself! Repeat this several times out loud, but for yourself, and then keep moving on with more statements to be filled. Next, repeat, "I love.…" and after finding and repeating your answer change to, "I hate…". Now that you have a bit more information about this character, the group interaction begins. Characters begin to greet each other and can now introduce themselves with the name they discovered. They also know what they love and hate, which can lead to further improvised dialogue. The leader, after allowing the characters to interact with each other for a bit of time, observes when there are some improvised conversations flowing, and calls out, "Freeze!" Everyone remains in character and allows the "freeze" to stop their actions, but does so without undue tension. The leader then "unfreezes" one duo or small group that may have been improvising together and lets them continue their conversation. This allows participants to now take their characters to a performance level since they have an audience. Side-coaching may include, "We need to hear you. Be sure you are projecting your voice. Really listen and respond to each other, receive what they are saying and conveying so you are interacting". After a short time, the leader will call out "freeze" to this team and then continue unfreezing groups until everyone has had a chance to have their improvisation featured. These improvisations can continue onward with varying moveable centers – always returning to the artistic center with the knowledge that those other characters are always available via their unique centers.

Discussion/Reflection

What types of characters emerged by utilizing these centers? How did these centers influence the interactions with others? What happened to your center while interacting? What happened to your interactions and dialogue when you were featured?

Improvisation 6: Centers via the audience

For these improvisations a duo goes up before the rest of the participants and is given a scenario – a place, a relationship, and a situation. As an example, the characters are two chefs who work together, in their restaurant kitchen, and must decide what to create for a celebrity dinner. Now the twist to this is that the audience gets to give them their centers for these characters. The leader requests a location, then a quality/image and a sense of movement for the first chef and then for the second chef. Anything goes and the actors must simply dive in and go with whatever they are given and let that dictate their character while still pursuing the given objective in the scenario. For this example, let's say that for chef #1, audience members called out left elbow, cotton candy, and swirling. For chef #2, audience members called out right hip, ocean waves, and crashing. The actors then proceed, and these centers will allow them to create unique characters that are trying to figure out what to make for their celebrity clients – usually with quite hilarious results.

Discussion/Reflection

Were you successful working with the random centers that were given to you? Did a certain type of character emerge for you? As audience members, what were the characters you observed and how did they interact? Could any aspect of the center be further emphasized for more of a transformation?

Improvisation 7: Text with improvised centers

The exercise above can now be used with memorized text, a scene that actors may be working with, but with the same improvised centers. Once again, it's fun to allow the audience to dictate what these centers will be, so that the actors are thrown into a new situation with their text. This is an excellent improv for removing staid line readings and getting actors to make new discoveries.

Discussion/Reflection

At the end of this scene, the actors are encouraged to fly back over what happened, while working from a positive mindset. The leader can ask each actor, "What did you appreciate overall with how this exercise went?" Be sure to steer the actors toward appreciation as often we are our own worst critic, and that criticism can stifle creativity and confidence. This was, after all, an improvisation utilizing the script and therefore whatever happened was "perfect". Next, the leader asks, "Was there a jewel of a moment that you discovered during the improv? One sparkling, shining moment that stood out?" The answer could be something the individual being questioned experienced, something they observed in their scene partner, or something they experienced through the audience such as unexpected laughter or a gasp. Michael Chekhov talks about jewelry in his technique, referring to these often-unexpected moments that may come through in a rehearsal that are then retained as part of the performance due to their uniqueness. The final question the leader will ask is, "If you were to repeat this improv again, what would you do differently to make it even better?" The answers for this might range from committing more to the center that was given to listening more carefully to their scene partner. This question allows the actors a moment of self-reflection and a realization of how they can continue to improve. Peers in the audience should also be given an opportunity to reflect to the actors after the self-reflection, via these same guidelines. What did the audience appreciate overall? What were some of the sparkling jeweled moments they observed? Are there any ideas of how to make it even better? This line of questioning and response creates a supportive atmosphere that promotes exploration and creativity.

Improvisation 8: A trio of centers (contributed by Suzanne Schmidt, Professional actor, instructor at the Los Angeles Television and Film Academy, and certified teacher via NMCA)

The students play with a location, quality, and mobility for three different moveable centers, finding their name, voice, occupation, and passions. Each actor will identify their characters as number 1, 2, and 3. After they choose one of these characters to embody to begin, they are now given an improvisational situation which is heightened. Suggestions for these situations are stuck in an elevator or stranded on a raft in the middle of the ocean. In the midst of these characters all interacting with their situation, the leader yells out, "New choice!" If they started as character 1, their "new choice" will be character 2 or 3. The improvisation then continues right where we left off, but now with new characters. At another critical moment the leader once again yells out, "New choice!", and each actor's final character picks up the improvisation where it left off. If the improvisation is going well, the leader can call out "new choice" several times, allowing the actors to rotate back to one of their three characters.

Alternately, all three (or more) character choices could have the same identity with the same occupation etc., and yet the moveable center choices affect how they deal with the given scenario. This variation works well if the actors are working to make discoveries about a particular character they are playing in a scene or play.

Wrap up
Begin by finding your artistic center that brings you back to a feeling of being grounded, confident, and ready for anything. Then explore changing that center to create character, by assigning a location, quality, and

sense of movement. Experiment with the center being fully expressed to veiling, from free-form improvisation to improvising a center with a memorized text.

Solo application

Work with centers may be done in a classroom or in a workshop with others. Exploring these on your own will provide you with endless possibilities for characters, and allow you to be more flexible when receiving direction. Working on your own with a text, you could explore a variety of centers to determine what seems to work best. Of course, for an acting role, you may "veil" that center much more than you did during the improvisation exercises, depending on the genre of work you are doing.

Script application

When analyzing your character, discover where the center for them lies and what quality it has and what sense of movement it contains. Be sure to explore many options to discover your character's core center, and then map when that center may be altered throughout the script. Does your character become so intensely tied to another that their center travels to them? Does a situation change the mobility of the center as their whole being freezes with fear or undulates with joy? Let your imagination use the center as a jumping off point for your imagination to lead you through your character's journey.

Life application

Utilizing your artistic center in the upper chest and entering situations that might be challenging with this sense of energy radiating within you can provide security and confidence. What a terrific way of walking into a job interview, or on a first date, utilizing your imagination to ignite that ball of energy within the upper chest so that you can present the best "you" possible. When your energy is dragging, either physically or emotionally, charging this artistic center with sunny energy can bring you to a revitalized state of being.

FIGURE 9.1 Three actors lying on the floor. Photograph by Melis Derya White. Actors L to R: Luis Alfonso Castro, Arleth Lopez, Aslan Longoria

9
THE IMAGINARY BODY

"But although Creative Images are independent and changeable within themselves, although they are full of emotions and desires, you, while working on your parts, must not think that they will come to you fully developed and accomplished. They don't. To complete themselves, to reach the degree of expressiveness that would satisfy you, they will require your active collaboration".

Michael Chekhov, Describing Michael Chekhov, To the Actor, *Routledge*, revised, 2002, courtesy of the Michael Chekhov Estate

The exciting fact about your imagination is that it has no limits! You are in control, and anything is possible. Michael Chekhov worked with his students to harness this power of imagination, and this section allows you to create a character by imagining what that character's body might be – then letting that creation influence your behavior – from your walk and gestures to your voice. Students of Michael Chekhov remarked how he would grow taller before their very eyes – simply by believing in a new body. When working with Blair Cutting, at the Michael Chekhov Studio in New York City, I found him to be a very calm man. However, there were times when he would exert a great power and I can only assume it was due to his mastery of this concept of imaginary body – he could take on a new persona. Blair Cutting was able to model the concept of transformation, becoming something new, a trait which creative artists long for. If you were to be hired as an actor for a resident theatre company, playing a variety of roles within a production season, you would want to be sure to transform yourself into each distinct character you played. This technique of imaginary body allows you to transform yourself and therefore present to an audience a distinct character each time you perform. This transformation may be quite subtle, or perhaps all-encompassing, depending on what a script might require. There are many avenues to experiment with, whether solo or as part of a group, and the only requirement for success is an open imagination!

Improvisation 1: Free-form

For this exercise, you'll want to let your imagination go wild. If there is a leader, they can assist by calling out sections of the body on which you then concentrate, with each participant working individually. You can also experiment with this on your own. This type of working with your imagination may not suit you, and other exercises will follow that you may better relate to. Give this a try, and remember you can always pretend – or move onto the next exercise.

Imagine that there is an endless sphere of characters that exist out in the ethers beyond the earth's atmosphere, and they are all accessible to you. One of my beloved mentors, Mala Powers, would relate how Michael Chekhov would assure her that any character you ever need to play is within your grasp – you simply call upon your imagination to connect you. You may decide to close your eyes or bring your vision to a soft focus as you imagine connecting to that endless sphere of images and allowing one to become clear to you. As with so many of these exercises, don't judge, simply allow your imagination to pull out a character and know that it's the right one for you to create at the time. You may choose to be seated, standing, or lying on the floor – whichever position puts you into the most receptive state. Once a character starts to take form, bring your concentration to their feet. What are they wearing on their feet? Shoes, sandals, sneakers, high heels, barefoot or? Do they have high arches, flat feet, wide feet, rough feet, smooth feet? As you are seeing this picture in your imagination, move your feet in space slightly taking on the qualities that you are viewing. Next bring your focus to their legs. Do they have well developed leg muscles, slender legs, rough knees, bulging quadriceps? What are they wearing on their legs – pants, shorts, skirt, tights, leggings or? Move your legs slightly as via your imagination you take on these legs. Then focus on the character's hips. Are these hips wide, narrow, flexible, staid? Does this character tend to stand with hips leaning forward or to the back or centered? How does their clothing reach up to the waist just above the hips? Is there a belt? Are their pants worn below the waistline, on the waistline, just above the waistline? Gently move your hips in space as you imagine taking on these hips. Now focus on their torso. How is their posture? Do they lean forward, back, slightly to one side? What are the muscles of the torso of your character? Are the muscles well developed? Are the abdominals tight or loose? What are they wearing on this torso? What is the color or colors or pattern? Gently move the torso in space as you take on this character's torso. Now focus on the shoulders, arms, and hands of this character. Are the shoulders upright, strong, slouched forward? Are the arms muscular or slender? View the biceps, triceps, forearms, wrists, and hands of this character in your imagination. Are those arms long and graceful or short and stodgy? How about those hands – young supple skin or older wrinkled skin? Are the fingers long and extended or short and stubby? Are their arms covered with clothing or bare? Is there a watch, a bracelet, rings? Are the nails healthy, painted, chewed? Gently move the arms in space as you imagine taking on these arms that you are seeing. Now focus on the neck and head of this character. Is the next slight and long or short and muscular? Is there a necklace? See all the facets of the face – the lips, teeth, tongue, cheeks, nose, eyes, eye lashes eyebrows, ears, forehead, and scalp. See if the eyelashes are long or the lips puffy. Are the eyes wide or narrow and what is their color? Do they have hair and if so what color, shape, texture? Are they wearing anything on their head – a hat, a scarf, headband, turban? Gently move all parts of the neck and face as you take on all these new qualities. Once this new imaginary body is established, gently open your eyes, and see the world through a new lens – that of this character. Imagine you are also taking on the mind and thoughts of this character along with the body. Begin to move around the space and experiment with picking up objects and placing them back down, sitting and getting up, leaning – becoming aware of how this new body functions. From here you can then take this new body into the improvisations below which connect with other characters.

For some, reaching into an imagined sphere may prove difficult and images may not be readily available. Therefore, the following improvisations pull from defined images so that participants have something specific to call upon to inspire a new imaginary body.

Discussion/Reflection

How did working with your imagination allow you to transform into a character? What were this character's main traits? Remembering that there is no 'wrong', know that if this exercise was a challenge that using more concrete imagery for character creation may be much more successful for you.

Improvisation 2: Characters from nature

This exercise could be done individually, given as an assignment outside of a class or as a group, depending on time and space. For this exercise you will go out and "commune" with nature. This is a time to put your observation skills to work and contemplate all that you are seeing in the natural world. You'll want to pick an area that has a diverse landscape, so that you have access to the greatest variety of plants, trees, shrubs, flowers, and even weeds. Engage your imagination as you view these items and begin to wonder how they might be used to create character – how they would manifest if in human form. Make a list of adjectives, and ideally you can draw upon other terminology from the Michael Chekhov technique. Is this plant contracting or expanding? Does it seem to be pushing out of the ground or reaching to the sky? Can you imagine the roots as feet and leaves as hands – or how would you connect plant parts to your own body? Once you have chosen a plant, tree, flower, shrub, or any item you viewed growing outside, you'll want to use the list of adjectives you created to now bring this item into human form. You may work on your own or a leader can call out body parts as before to allow you to focus. You may be standing, sitting, or lying down – whatever position best supports you and your imagination. You'll work once again from the feet up to the top of your head, letting your body take on the qualities that you observed in your nature subject, now with a defined image that you observed as your inspiration. Once you have fully transformed yourself via your nature imagery, you will move through the space with this newly imagined body.

Alternative

If a varied landscape is not available to you, this exercise can be done via pictures or watching a video of a landscape and zeroing in on one plant or tree. This could also be achieved by having a leader bring into a class or workshop a stack of individual pictures of plants and have each participant study the picture to create an imaginary body.

Discussion/Reflection

Were you able to successfully use an item from nature as a springboard into a character? If so, what were the main traits that you grasped from the item and how did they manifest in the character?

Improvisation 3: The museum

Ideally for this exercise, you would visit a museum, which is often free on college campuses, and study the vast array of items there. Eventually you will pick one item which may be an artifact, a statue, or any of the many visual artistic images available and use that as your inspiration to character. Write down adjectives from your observation and then use those adjectives to inspire a new imaginary body. As before you will take the time to transform each section of your body, incorporating this new imagery and then moving as this new character. After you create your character, everyone can swap the lists of written traits and others will now use your list as a guide to create their own version of a character.

Discussion/Reflection

Were you able to utilize an item to transform into a character? What traits from the object did you incorporate into the character? If you did swap lists, how did your character change when taken on by another individual?

Improvisation 4: Portraits/photographs/cartoons

This exercise allows you to see another body and use that body as your springboard to create a new and distinct character. This may be done as part of a museum visit, with the focus on portraits displayed there, or via photographs from a magazine or via a visit to the library, and cartoons from online or printed sources. By observing all of these different characters and then taking on their qualities, your ability to create and believe in an imaginary body for yourself will greatly increase. A leader may choose to bring in portraits, photographs, or cartoons, and these could be geared toward a specific time in history or a genre of performance. A director may want to do this exercise with actors and provide portraits that represent the time period in which the play takes place, or if working on a farcical comedy, cartoon characters may help the actors bring the piece to life. Actors could also be asked to bring in their ideas of characters. For this exercise, a leader and participants will want to be aware of cultural sensitivity. While much can be said about viewing and then creating a character that is quite different from you, "walking in their shoes", agreement would be needed from the group for this exercise. If acceptable, portraits representing a variety of ethnicities, cultures, sexual identities, ages, and genders could be shuffled and distributed for creation. If a participant was uncomfortable with the portrait received, they could trade for another. A discussion prior to this exercise may be needed to establish that the group takes care with characters outside of their cultural/racial identity in order to prevent offenses to others, and to mirror casting in the industry. This exercise could also proceed with all of the portraits displayed and each participant can then view and choose the character they'd like to create. Participants could also bring their own portraits to class, with the instruction that they want to create a character very different from themselves. This is NOT a casting exercise, since casting has very specific parameters and works for the most ideal representation for the characters in a script, but instead this is an exercise to stretch your limitations, to engage your imagination, and to enjoy and empathize with a character that is very different from yourself. Again, there must be consent in the group regarding creating this variety of characters.

While you can guide yourself through this exercise, having a leader guide your focus so you can be more exacting with the creation of the imaginary body is preferable. Ideally participants will lie on their backs, though however they are most comfortable is acceptable of course. Next, everyone studies their picture, closing their eyes periodically and testing if they can fully view this character in their mind. If the portrait is incomplete, perhaps just showing a torso, you will want to imagine the rest of this character in detail – filling in any blanks. If the portrait is in black and white, then you will want to imagine the character in color. Once you feel that you can see your character in detail with your eyes closed, turn your picture upside down next to you. This will be the signal for the leader to proceed with instructions. For this exercise, some instructions will be given for you to release your own personal tensions – this series can also be used for other character creation methods if effective for you. Bring your concentration to your own two feet. Now squeeze all the muscles of the feet, from the toes to the heels – good and tight – then completely release. Allow your feet to sink into the earth beneath you. Next, focus on the legs and hips from the ankles all the way up to the waist. Imagine all the parts of you making up this area – shins, calves, knees, thighs, pelvic area, and glutes. Once your focus is there, squeeze all those body parts tightly. Glutes squeeze and raise you off the floor a bit, quadriceps, hamstrings and calves all tight, pelvis is squeezed…and then totally released. Imagine this lower half of your body sinking into the earth, fully supported by the earth – no need to hang onto anything. Next, bring your focus to your torso, imagining all the varied areas from the abdominals to all the vertebrae of the spine, rib cage, and pectoral muscles. Now tighten all those muscles – abs pulled in, rib cage squeezing…and then completely release. Let the earth support your torso – no effort needed. Next, bring your focus to your shoulders, arms, and hands – then squeeze all those muscles – biceps, triceps, forearms, hands, and fingers – then completely release, letting your arms be fully supported by the earth. Next bring your focus to your neck, face, and head. Visualize all the muscles there – from those that move your cheeks and eyebrows right up to your scalp. Now tighten the neck, face, and entire head… all your features scrunched – then completely release, feeling your face gently melting away. Now bring your focus to your breath, allowing that breath to move freely to this released body. Imagine that with your personal tensions gone, and your body in a relaxed state, that you can more easily allow for the physicality of a new character. Now, bring that picture of your character back to the forefront of your mind. Michael Chekhov talks about images being purified by our subconscious, and perhaps the picture you now see is a bit different – that is perfect. Let it be – no need to consult your actual picture again – let your imagination guide you. As if you are a camera that can zoom, bring your attention to the character's feet. See these feet in detail and then imagine inhaling these feet with deep breath and as you exhale, drop these feet onto your own. You now have the character's feet. Proceed with the zoom lens for all parts of this character's body – inhaling each image and then exhaling as you drop that body part onto your own. Once you have the body established you can then rise from the floor with this new body – it might be a way that you would not move so it's time to make a discovery!

Discussion/Reflection

How did this exercise work for you? Was it helpful to be guided in the release of your own personal tensions so that you had a blank slate to then create your new imaginary body? Was it helpful to work on one body part at a time with the breath for your creation? Were you able to clearly see the image of your character in your mind after studying your picture? Did your character morph at all when you then brought it back to mind – perhaps altered by your subconscious?

Improvisation 5: Animals

Working with animal imagery has been a classic theatre exercise and animals provide a terrific springboard to creating an imaginary body. Once an animal is chosen, either from the imagination, live observation, or photographs, you will then explore moving just as that animal moves. This may mean lying on the floor and slithering like a snake, or literally hopping like a rabbit. Once the actual moves have been explored, you'll want to "veil" these movements and bring your character to standing and moving through the space as human. However, vestiges of what you discovered should remain. Maybe the snake character slightly undulates the spine as they walk. The rabbit may have a bounce in their step. Take the time to explore all the ways that this imaginary body, inspired by an animal, moves in the space – from picking up objects, sitting, leaning, and relating to everything around them.

Discussion/Reflection

Did you feel that you completely inhabited the body of your chosen animal? What were the major traits you discovered? Were you able to translate those traits into human behavior? What did you determine was the leading center for this character? Did you find a quality and sense of movement for that center? Could you relate your discovery to a character type?

Improvisation 6: Time to interact

Using any of the above springboards which lead to the creation of an imaginary body, a leader will guide a group in their individual creations. Once everyone is moving around the space with their imagined body, which may have been gained via a nature observation, a portrait, an animal, or any other creative source, the focus now settles on the breath. How is the breath operating in this new body? Is the breath deep, shallow, noisy, silent? Once the breath is noted, make a touch of sound on your exhalation. Surprise yourself with this voice as it is now an extension of the imaginary body you created. It may be higher, lower, more nasal, or breathier than your typical voice. You will want to be sure that you support the voice with an open throat so that you create the voice in a healthy way. Once the sound is established, then let a greeting come to you from this new imaginary body which is now becoming a unique character. Again, surprise yourself – perhaps your greeting is gibberish. If that is what organically comes to you then so be it. The point is to let your choices emanate from this imaginary body, rather than forcing yourself to be different or unique in this moment. The imaginary body by its nature will provide you with this unique character. Once you've practiced your greeting, exchange that greeting with everyone you pass by. Perhaps your greeting also includes a gesture – a wave, an impulse to fist bump, to shake hands, or any way that your new character behaves. As was done with the characters created via moveable centers, a leader can feed you open-ended statements and allow you to fill in the blanks, inspired by your new character. Repeat out loud for yourself: My name is...., I love...., I hate.... My biggest dream is...., and spontaneously let answers come to you. Once these are established, which allows a personality to begin to develop for this character, begin to improvise with those around you. You can begin by sharing what you learned from the statements, but then let that flow into conversation. A leader can then freeze the group as has been done in previous exercises, and then unfreeze duos or smaller groups that are interacting, so everyone gets to view what's happening with these new characters.

Discussion/Reflection

Did you find specific gestures for your character as you imagined situations? Did the leading statements lead you to further discoveries? Did your answers then inform how you interacted with other characters? Were you able to let the dialogue flow as you continued to improvise?

Improvisation 7: "Ani-morphosis" (contributed by Geoffrey Arndt, Theatre Director and Instructor at the Chicago's Loyola Academy, Certified Teacher via NMCA)

In this exercise, we will explore Imaginary Bodies through different animals. To begin, connect with your ideal artistic center, and reach up into an imagined sphere of images to pull down a single image of an animal of your choice. Allow the image of the animal to fill up the various parts of your body and begin to move. Exploring how this animal can affect the way you move your arms, legs, torso, as well as how it affects your breath. As you gain confidence with your new body, begin to interact with the environment around you. Then, greet those around you. The instructor is invited to introduce tasks that you might complete in this new body, such as taking a drink, laying down to go to sleep and waking up, and playing a specific game. After exploring these tasks, create a scene where there is a clear conflict and each actor must choose animals that may have a natural polarity with each other: dog and cat, for instance. Scenes could begin with one actor engaged in a physical activity that might interest a specific animal: a beaver could be building something. Consider how an elephant might make a peanut butter and jelly sandwich as a parakeet enters to ask for their car keys.

Wrap up

Using your imagination and various springboards from nature to historical artifacts to pictures, enjoy transforming yourself into a variety of characters, fully investing in their animation. Allow your characters to interact and explore further development of their personalities, via your answers to open-ended statements and relating to the other characters around you.

Solo application

You can continue to create characters and allow yourself to experiment with transformation, either purely through your imagination or with a variety of springboards. When working alone, you might spot an item, recognize that item's dominant traits and then incorporate them in order to transform yourself into a character.

Script application

As you study your character, delve into your imagination to discover what images are there that relate to your character. A seemingly abstract connection, such as your character as a daisy or a stone, can inspire you to transform yourself by using traits in the imagery you choose. Depending on the genre and style of your script, these traits may be more overt or extremely subtle, but provide you with something defined to spring into character.

Life application

These exercises develop our imagination and curiosity, which can apply to any aspect of life. We all play many parts in our lives and being able to relate to everything around us and incorporate the traits that we see and experience, allows us to be more flexible and adaptable. You may need the solidness of a rock or the gentleness of a daisy petal in certain situations, and you can engage with your imagination to be the best you.

FIGURE 10.1 Five actors wearing various costume pieces, wigs, hats. Photograph by Melis Derya White. Actors L to R: Omar Moreno, Luis Alfonso Castro, Arleth Lopez, Shawn Pirkle, Aslan Longoria

10
COSTUME CHARACTERS

"With his mother and nanny as audience, he would don a hat, a scarf, any available, odd piece of clothing and at once began to improvise. He became a different child, a new character – sometimes tragic, sometimes so humorous that his nanny would rock back and forth with laughter, until tears rolled down her cheeks".

Mala Powers, Describing Michael Chekhov, To the Actor, *Routledge Press*, revised, 2002, courtesy of the Michael Chekhov Estate

Whether or not you played with clothing items as a child and improvised characters, no doubt you can recognize how fun that could be. While some actors have a wonderful career based on their personalities, Michael Chekhov focused his work on creating transformation in the actor, and costumes can aid that transformation. If you think about known actors, you can most likely come up with a list of those that are successful due to their personalities, and those that seem to transform into a different character with every part they play. There is no judgment as both ways of working can lead to success and entertain an audience, but most actors do enjoy playing against "type". In fact, many actors have spoken about how they got into the profession to become someone else. Stories have circulated about how some actors are quite shy in private, but when it comes time to perform, they transform into the creative artists that the public recognizes. This is a talent in itself, and the more you play with the transformative process, the more adept you will become at finding variety in the characters you play.

The method behind these exercises is to use a costume element as a springboard to total transformation. Professional actors have often reported that they have not truly felt themselves as the character until they are in the costume. The costume helps any actor to fully transform and enter the fictitious world of the play. This is especially true with period pieces when costumes of the era are nothing like modern day clothing and therefore create a completely different ambience when worn. Costumes can also influence your way of walking, standing, sitting – your repertoire of movement. While a full costume is often unavailable until close to a show opening, an excellent policy is to wear the character shoes as early as possible – or some facsimile of that footwear. From bare feet, to sandals, to heeled boots, to canvas sneakers – they all inspire a different way of moving and posture. For these exercises, a bevy of costume items is needed and can be obtained via collecting cast-offs from costume shops, or trips to salvage stores and garage sales. For very little money, a terrific array of clothing can be assembled which will allow for an entire world of characters to emerge.

Improvisation 1: Creative costumes

This could be done solo on your own, or if working with a group, in your own individual space, working to enhance your creativity. If working in a group, a variety of costume pieces are put on display in the middle of the space to begin. The leader will ask everyone to circle around this display of items and begin engaging your imagination as you look at what is on display before you. Take a moment to look at each item and imagine who might wear that item and what their life is like. Continue to look through all the items as time allows, conjuring up images of various characters. When the leader claps, or gives a predetermined signal, each person grabs just one of the items. You may have had your eye on something, but it will be the luck of the draw and the quickness of the grab which will determine if you get that item. However, any item can inspire your creativity. Once you have your item, turn your back to the circle and start to work with this item of clothing. There is a typical way that it is to be worn, and you may start with that. Once you have it placed onto yourself, begin to move in your own space a bit like that character, imagining and incorporating their walk, their gestures, and being in their life for a few moments. Once you have an inkling of who that character might be, keep the costume piece in motion, trying it over different body parts and letting it become other than it was originally intended to be. A vest might now become a turban, a diaper, a sling, a leg bandage…. Let your imagination go wild. If you are feeling stuck, simply move the item onto different body parts and often that action will inspire a new way of wearing this costume. Continue to move the costume around, finding as many characters as possible.

Discussion/Reflection

Did you surprise yourself with the way that you were able to use the costume piece that was not in line with its original intent? What variety of characters were you able to express with the one costume piece you employed?

Improvisation 2: Walk the runway

For this improvisation, the group divides up into teams with perhaps a trio depending on numbers. There must be either a large array of costume items that everyone can utilize, or each team could be given a grouping of items. One team member agrees to be the model and the other(s) will be the fashion stylists for the runway. The stylist now begins to place the costume pieces on the model, as if creating a unique sculpture. Once the model is in costume, the stylists now act as directors, giving the model character prompts. Perhaps this model walks with an uplifted chin at a very slow pace. Perhaps they walk with a very rhythmic step akin to a wedding march and take plenty of pauses to show off what they are wearing. The model incorporates these prompts to create their character, allowing their entire physicality to alter depending upon what is given by the stylist(s). The ideal is to allow the model to become quite different from their everyday self, thereby having fun transforming into a character that is unlike them. Once this is established and the stylists have coached the model on their walk and behavior, the fashion show begins. A runway area is determined, and each model walks that runway one at a time while the stylist act as the announcers, telling the audience about their model and the wonderful fashion they are wearing. If there is a microphone for the announcers and some background music, this makes this improv even more fun and entertaining. After all the initial models have finished walking the runway, the teams switch, with the stylists now becoming the model, and the exercise repeats.

Discussion/Reflection

Stylists: was it easy or a challenge to figure out the character of your model once you had them dressed? Did you make changes as you went along to create a more unique character?

Models: how easy was it to accept the stylist's direction for your character? Did you add your own flair and if so, how did you enhance what you were given? What was your confidence walking the runway? Did having a determined character allow you to walk the runway with more ease?

Improvisation 3: Costume character interaction

Once everyone has had a chance to work on their own with a costume piece, and as a character by being a model, it's time to bring these characters together. This could be an assignment where each participant has worked on creating a character on their own via a costume piece and brings it to the group or is done as a group via the exercise above. Each person now chooses one way to wear their costume item, perhaps the way that inspired them the most, and then begins to walk in the space. Be aware that you may now walk at a completely different tempo and perhaps there is a defined rhythm to your walk. You may be looking around at the world in a different way. Let this costume item completely transform you. The item doesn't just affect the area of the body on which it's worn but the whole body. The cloth that becomes a veil over the face influences you all the way down to your toes. You want 100 percent of the body engaged in this transformation. As you walk, connect with your breath. How is your breathing different now because of this new costume character? On your next exhalation, take a touch of sound and surprise yourself with your new voice. Imagine your voice is magically transformed by this costume piece and the character that is emerging. As with other previous character exercises, a leader can now feed you leading sentences for which you fill in the blank. Begin with, "My name is…". Let an answer just pop in for you. No need to think – just continue to move as the character and repeat the phrase out loud for yourself and when a name pops in, repeat the whole phrase so you begin to get comfortable with your "new" voice. Continue with several other phrases, taking time with each one and letting something fill in from your new character, "I love…", "I hate…", and "My favorite person is…". As has been done with character work before, bring all these characters into a circle. One at a time, go around the circle, and each character will say their name and whatever they remember of what they love, hate, and a favorite person. After everyone has had a chance to speak, these characters are given the instruction to find another character across the circle that you feel you may relate to. Perhaps you both love or hate the same thing, or you were intrigued when they spoke about their favorite person. Other prompts may include, "Find the character in the room with whom you feel most safe and comfortable and strike up a conversation" or "Find the character in the room who makes you feel most uncomfortable and see if you can discover why". The characters then move into duos or groups and begin improvised interaction. After these interactions are established, the leader will call out "Freeze!" and then signal to one team at a time to come back "alive" so everyone can get a glimpse into their conversation. This repeats until all teams have a chance to be heard.

Discussion/Reflection

How did the costume piece assist you in creating this character? How did finding answers to the open-ended statements help in creating your character? Did you surprise yourself with any of your character's answers? How did you maintain your character as you interacted?

Improvisation 4: What you want right now!

As before, every student should choose a costume piece, work with it around the body, and then decide upon the final way of wearing it. Each participant then begins to move about the space, discovering their costume character's walk and posture, and breath. Once again let a touch of sound out during the exhalation and let yourself be surprised and accept whatever sound is produced. Once a voice is established, open-ended statements are once again given as before such as, "My name is…", "I love…", "I hate…", "My favorite food is…", "My favorite place is…", and then an important one for this improv, "What I want right now is…". After you have established these bits of personality for your new character, everyone now lines up shoulder to shoulder, all facing in one direction, with a space directly in front where there is ample room to perform. Now the character from one end and the character from the other end of the line walk in front of everyone into the "performance space" and begin to improvise. They know their names and can introduce themselves, and they know their loves and hates, and they know what they want right now. The objective of each character is to get what they want from the other character. Basic improv guidelines apply which are to always say yes, and…not denying whatever is set up by the other character but somehow working with it. It may be that you are in two completely different eras and somehow you will respond to whatever makes sense from your era. Maybe you are a time traveler? You want to see if you can get what you want which can lead to the conclusion of this encounter. Are you at a stalemate and you each turn away and return to opposite ends of the line? Do you reach an agreement, and you happily exit together as a duo? Any result is perfect. As this team is exiting, the next two characters on either end of the line now start to enter the performance space and begin their interaction, working with their objective – getting what they want right now! This could be as simple as a snack you are craving or as deep as true love. The fun is in the discoveries between the two characters. Once this duo has reached some sort of conclusion they exit and the improv continues with two characters entering the performance space, down the line until everyone has had the opportunity to present. If there is an odd number, the leader can encourage anyone who would like to go to repeat. After everyone has gone, imagine that your costume piece has magical properties and that once you remove it, the character instantly disappears. There is never any need to hold onto a character, but instead know that they are available to draw upon at any time in the future.

COSTUME CHARACTERS 127

Discussion/Reflection

Did adding an intention/objective, your character's want in the moment assist with the improvisation? Were you able to stay committed to your characterization while still accepting the reality of whomever you played opposite to? Did you feel a sense of entirety/wholeness as you found a conclusion to your improvised scene? What elements may have made your improvised interaction even stronger?

Improvisation 5: Presenting solo as a trio

This is an opportunity to improvise in front of peers using costume pieces to inspire "instant" characters. Three costume items are put in front of the audience, with other items that are available such as a chair, table, and a few props.

Version 1

The leader places the costume items in full view of everyone participating. Participants then activate their imaginations as they consider who might be wearing each item. After a short time, the first volunteer can go forward and wear the first item, letting what they imagined come to life. The dialogue is completely improvised, and they may present it as a private inner monologue or break the fourth wall and talk directly to the audience – their choice. After the first character is established, that costume piece is removed and the character disappears with that piece, and now the second costume piece is worn and a new character emerges, and then eventually onto the third one. If there is time to incorporate this improvisation more than once, you can then work on incorporating the Four Brothers of Art into the exercise, particularly creating a beginning, middle, and end with some sort of through line to the story of these three characters. This exercise is a great starting point for creating a one-person show and could be a challenging final project for a class – three distinct characters depicting a coherent story. With more practice, ease will enter the exercise and if rehearsed rather than improvised then more detailed form can emerge, with the artistic beauty of the piece shining through via immersion into the exercise.

Version 2

For more of a challenge, a volunteer can enter the performance space without knowing what the three clothing items will be. Instead, the leader will draw from a pile after the performer is in front of the audience and randomly place the items near the performer. The performer will then instantly grab a costume item and wear it in the way that their imagination provides in that moment. If after the choice being made the performer feels it's awkward, all the better! This is what improvisation is all about – being in the moment with whatever is happening – even if it was your choice. The performer remains with their initial instinct and starts to speak and move like that character. As before, once that character is established, and the exercise is brought to an end, the costume piece is removed; another item can then be chosen and a new character created.

Version 3

This version utilizes someone from the audience to call out directions. This can work in two different ways. More than three costume items are placed in the playing area and a volunteer comes forward. The audience member that has been designated now calls out which item the performer will wear first, which might be "Jacket!" or "Hat!" The performer grabs the item, wears it in whatever way their imagination may provide them in that moment, and begins to bring a character alive. When the caller from the audience feels that character has been established, they call out "End!" and the performer brings that character to an ending point and removes the costume piece. As soon as that item is removed, the caller from the audience prompts the performer to pick up the next item they designate, and the improvisation continues. This can stop after three items as in the previous improvs, or perhaps go on to four, or five, or more as more of a challenge.

Improvisation 6: The interview (contributed by Christie Maturo, theatre professor at Central Connecticut State University, professional actor, and NMCA certified teacher of the Michael Chekhov technique)

What is needed:

- A variety of costume pieces (hats, vests, skirts, scarves, etc..)
- Table, two chairs
- Four slips of paper/person, pen, or pencil
- Two bowls/receptacle for holding slips of paper, recycle bin

The set up

Each student is given four slips of paper. On one sheet, they should write the name of a place where a person might be interviewing for a job and a position that makes sense for that location (for example: Lincoln High School, PE teacher, or Hilton Hotel, concierge).

On each of the three other sheets, they are to write one question per sheet. These questions could be questions that might come up in a job interview such as, "What qualities do you possess that would make you a good candidate for this position?". Or these could be questions that might be completely unrelated to a job interview, such as, "Do you like scary movies, why or why not?" To maximize fun, encourage students to write questions that will elicit more than just a simple yes or no response.

Have students fold all their pieces of paper in half and collect all the job locations/positions in one receptacle and collect the questions in another. Set these aside for the moment.

The costume

Lay out costume pieces and ask students to select one. Have students "wear" the costume piece in a variety of different ways. For example, they might try the scarf around the neck, then over the head, or around the waist, or wrapped around their hands as if in a muff…Often the most fun choice to explore isn't always the first one that comes to mind, so encourage them to play.

After some time, ask the students to wear the costume piece in the way that they found to be the most fun. Have them move around the room, or sit, or explore in their own capacity the way the costume piece influences their movement and/or the way in which they carry their body and how they view the world. Encourage them to follow their impulses without judgment or fear of doing it "wrong".

Announce that on the count of three, everyone should say their character's name aloud. Whatever comes out is perfect! Feel free to ask the class other questions about their characters, such as, "What is your greatest fear?" or, "What is your favorite song?" or "Do you have a catch phrase?"

The improv

Two students at a time will take the space wearing their costume piece and portraying the character they just created. One person is seated at the table with the two bowls of folded paper in front of them. The other student will enter. The student entering is here for a job interview. The person seated at the table is the interviewer.

The characters may introduce themselves/make pleasantries. Then the interviewer will draw from the bowl of job locations and position description. They will welcome the interviewee to the place and inform them of the position they are interviewing for. Allow any improv to occur.

When ready, the interviewer will draw a total of three questions, asking each in turn. Being led by the characters they created, the interviewee will improvise answers. Give the performers time to play and explore. The improvisation will conclude when the interviewer says something to the effect of, "You're hired", "Don't call us, we'll call you", "Thank you for coming in, but this doesn't seem to be a great fit", "Not a chance in hell!", etc. At the end of the improv, the actors involved should make sure to recycle/remove their used job descriptions and questions, so that the same ones aren't being drawn again and again.

Variations

Once each pair has had a chance to go once, you can reshuffle the pairs (or keep them the same) and have the interviewers become the interviewees. Students may choose to swap a costume piece with someone and create a new character instantly. Pairs may swap costume pieces and use the new piece to make a character different from what their improv partner created.

Wrap up

Be creative with costume pieces by using them not only as they were intended to be worn, but in other creative ways that lead to unique characters. By modeling, interacting, and creating instant characters via the imagination, your skill with characterization will grow.

Solo application

Have fun playing with clothing items at home and letting your imagination expand with each item you explore – who might be wearing this? Also observe others in life and what they are wearing and how that helps define their character for you from a visual perspective.

Script application

In a production you will typically have a costume designer who will work with the director's concept and analyze the characters to create costumes. Sometimes you may be able to have input but if not, do study what will be given to you to incorporate the costume into your character choices. If there is not a designer, then analyze your character to decide what you will be wearing and wear the shoes of the character as soon as possible in rehearsal.

Life application

Enjoy playing your everyday roles and how they are altered depending on the costume you are wearing. Dressing in jogging shorts will allow you a completely different way of being than a gown or three-piece suit while attending a wedding. Enjoy these moments of playing your parts in life with the costume pieces you choose each day. You may discover that depending on the costume you choose to wear, your behavior and resulting experiences may be altered. Allowing yourself to be playful and appreciate your own style will enhance your creativity and allow you to model that sense of joy for others.

FIGURE 11.1 Three actors, one in chair in thinking pose. Photograph by Melis Derya White. Actors L to R: Luis Alfonso Castro, Omar Moreno, Arleth Lopez

11

THINKING, FEELING, AND WILLING

THE TRINITY OF THE PSYCHOLOGY

> *"Each of us knows that every normal human being exercises three main psychological functions: thoughts, feelings and will impulses".*
> Michael Chekhov, To the Actor, *Routledge Press, revised, 2002, courtesy of the Michael Chekhov Estate*

One of the initial questions that Michael Chekhov would ask actress Mala Powers when coaching her on a role was whether her character was predominately thinking, feeling, or willing. While we embody all these elements, when creating a role, choosing one of these as a predominant way of operating in the world can lead to a wonderous transformation into character. In this chapter you will work with specific movements that can assist you in contacting these variations of yourself, such as moving in a very linear fashion as a thinking character, in a circular pattern when feeling, and at angles as a willing character. While in our everyday life it is helpful to balance these, so we aren't guided solely by sheer will, or feelings, but that we also think things through. However, for character creation it's much more interesting to find an imbalance and experience what that may bring to a performance.

The concept behind this technique is that you can make each character you portray unique by determining if they are predominantly a thinking character, a feeling character, or a will-force character. In life we are a combination of all of these – our will force is what gets us out of bed in the morning, even if we didn't get enough sleep but we know we have tasks to accomplish. Our thinking forces allow us to rationalize right and wrong and to sort out complex issues. Our feeling force allows us to respond to stimuli and determine for ourselves what we enjoy and what we prefer to avoid. We need all these psychological elements to function in the world, but choosing to have a predominance of one of these will create unique characters. For exercise purposes, we will exaggerate these forces physically and vocally, but later "veiling" them can lead to unique and more subtle choices for character.

Improvisation 1: Thinking

Try multiplying in your head 468 × 723. Do not give up, even if math is not your forte. Truly attempt to do this calculation with as much concentration as you can give it. After a short while, ask yourself – where was my dominant energy during that task – most likely you'll report that it was in your head, your mind. Did you note any gestures you were making? Perhaps you were using your fingers to try and calculate or writing with your fingers in the air as if on an imaginary blackboard, or maybe you were pressing keys on an invisible calculator. All of these are clues to the behavior of a thinking dominated character. Energy is centered in the head and energy is strong in the digits – both with the digits being calculated and the digits which are your fingers. Did you find yourself moving in space during this calculation? If so, how were you moving? You may have noted that you paced back and forth in a straight line which can be very typical when trying to think through a problem or situation.

Now begin to move through space, keeping these ideas in mind. Move in a very linear pattern, making straight lines in space. When you turn, turn with very sharp right angles. Tap your forehead or temple with your index finger. Analyze objects in the space by walking directly toward them and pointing at them with your index finger. Rest your elbow on your wrist joint and the knuckles of the opposite hand under your chin.

If your balance is strong, rest your ankle on top of the opposite knee joint and sink a bit into that pose. Is this familiar? It's no coincidence that Rodin's sculpture "The Thinker" is using this joint-on-joint arrangement. From this you can determine that there is a universality to this thinking energy, and it will be recognized by an audience. As you continue to examine items in the space, start to speak out loud about the items. This is an opportunity to let your voice respond with the precision that has been established by focusing on thinking. Taking the elements that you are now aware of – the straight lines, sharp angles, and joint-on-joint relationships of the body for gesture, your vocal articulation can mirror these qualities. Allow your diction to be very sharp, moving your lips in a strong linear way and pressing them together to make plosives such as your *p* and *b* strong and clear. The tongue can press strongly behind the upper teeth for your *t*'s, and *d*'s and the tongue can strongly connect to the roof of your mouth to medial sounds such as the *k*. The result should be very crisp and clear diction for this thinking character. For more detail on sounds associated with thinking, feeling, and willing, consult the *Michael Chekhov Playbook* (Lisa Dalton is the primary author), available in online stores or through NMCA.

Improvisation 2: Feeling

To begin to discover a connection to this aspect of your psychology, find an object that has meaning to you, that has a story behind it that you feel is quite special. Examine that object and remember the significance of that object. Let yourself move in space as you examine the object and recall its significance. Once you have spent a bit of time with this item that is precious to you, determine where your energy seems to be. You may note that the energy seems to be centered in the chest area – the resting place of the heart. When you were moving through space and perhaps in moving your object, did you note any particular pattern? The pattern associated with feeling is one of curves – much softer than the linear pattern of thinking. Were you examining your object with an open palm? Allowing your palms to be open and exposing the more tender part of the arms, the inner side, will allow you to connect to the feeling part of you. Begin to speak out loud about this object. In order to allow feeling to flow, let your vowels be fully expressed – perhaps even elongated a bit, enjoying the round sounds as you move with curves in the space.

Improvisation 3: The will force

You may have heard parents talk about the terrible twos – that age when toddlers begin to exert their will force and they want what they want. You now have the joy of returning for a moment in your imagination to your two-year-old self, imagining that you have been denied whatever it was you wanted…an ice cream cone, a ride on a swing…and throw a complete tantrum about it! Express yourself however you see fit in order to get what you want – right now! Let your feet express this will, your arms, your hands, your jaw – all of you wants what you want! You now have the clues to create a character that is dominated by will. Imagine strength in the heels of the feet, the heels of the hands, expressive thumbs, and a strong, iron jaw. You may have noticed a tendency to dig in your heels or that you kept your fists closed with only your thumb out. You may have been strongly pouting and jutting your jaw forward. Take that energy that you found as a two-year-old and bring it into adulthood and imagine expressing something you want. Keep the vulnerable palms hidden and emphasize gestures with your thumbs. Let that muscular jaw affect your speech giving you a more guttural, plosive sound as you chew out your words. Let your movements in space and gestures take on strong angles, which can go in any direction – no longer the lines of the thinking character or the curves of the feeling pattern. Your movements now go any which way to get what you want done!

Improvisation 4: The Wizard of Oz (archetypes)

Most of us are familiar with the story of the "Wizard of Oz", so the characters from that story/film will be used for this improvisation. Teams are assembled with one person playing the part of either Dorothy or the Wizard, and the other character to be either the Scarecrow, Lion, or Tin Man. Whether Dorothy or the Wizard, the question to pursue from the other character will be. "What do you want?" Continue to question your fellow character, allowing them to get more specific and to answer the "why" when they let you know what it is they want. For those very familiar with the story, they may even use actual quotes from the characters.

If there are those unfamiliar with the story, then spending a bit of time reviewing it will be helpful. The Scarecrow, Lion, and Tin Man tell Dorothy or the Wizard what it is they want, why they want it, and how it might change their circumstances. After the teams have some time to improvise, discussion ensues.

Discussion/Reflection 1

What is it that each character wanted? How did these relate to thinking, feeling, and willing? If you were Dorothy or the Wizard, what did you note about the other character's behavior? Did any of that behavior fit into the archetypal movement that is associated with the aspect of psychology they displayed? Hopefully it becomes obvious that the Scarecrow wanting a brain relates to thinking, the Tin Man wanting a heart to feeling, and the lion wanting courage to will force.

Replay

After the discussion and realizing how these iconic characters relate to the trinity of the psychology, use the archetypal movements to improvise the same interviews (this may also be a time to change characters). Allow the Scarecrow to move in a linear fashion with joint-on-joint gestures and emphasizing pointing with the index finger and using precise articulation of speech; allow the Tin Man to move in a circular pattern, with curving gestures in the area of the heart and an emphasis on open vowels while speaking; allow the lion to move without a pattern, focusing on a center in the hips and letting the speech take on a guttural sound.

Discussion/Reflection 2

Did the application of the movement and voice associated with each aspect of psychology allow the characters to be played differently? Were you able to relate to the various aspects of psychology? As the interviewers, what differences did you notice in this round?

Improvisation 5: Creating a new hospital

For this improvisation, everyone imagines that they are all board members who will be making decisions about a new hospital which is about to break ground. A hospital has been chosen as typically this will bring up very strong ideas since health care is a constant issue for so many. Before the improv begins, everyone is assigned a number, 1, 2, or 3. Students with Number 1 are then informed they will be thinking characters, students with Number 2 will be feeling characters, and students with Number 3 will be will-driven characters. Everyone then mingles at this "social event" for the hospital board, sharing their thoughts and ideas about the project. As you can imagine, many differing ways of looking at the new hospital will arise. Be sure and allow the varied forces to influence your character's behavior and their discussion agenda. Once the improvisation is underway, the leader can freeze the group and then signify one team to "unfreeze" so everyone can witness what happens as the variety of characters discuss their ideas. It may be that a thinker and a feeling character work to negotiate their wants for the project. Perhaps two will-centered characters create a timeline that they want the group to follow. It's all perfect, as the improvised ideas will come via the creative artistry of the group and the inspiration that using this trinity of psychology can offer.

Discussion/Reflection

What were the thinking characters most focused on? What were the intentions of the feeling characters? How did the will force characters behave and what were their priorities?

Improvisation 6: Party planning

This is an opportunity to share with a team member the same aspect of their psychology as they plan a party together. If this is done with a production cast, they may plan the party for the final night. Perhaps someone in the group has an upcoming birthday they could plan for. Any impetus for a party will start the conversation rolling. The group is divided up into teams of two, and a team of three if an odd number, and they are given one aspect from the trinity of psychology. Let's decide that everyone will be thinking characters. The teams now plan between themselves the ultimate party, from this intellectual bent. The teams should utilize all of the information learned from earlier explorations such as crisps diction, index finger point, gestures that refer to the head, joint-on-joint positions such as with the Rodin sculpture, and movements that are direct and linear. Once the teams have had a bit of time to come up with a plan, each team shares with the group their thoughts for the ultimate party.

Next, it's back to the party planning but now everyone is a feeling dominated character. This means that movements will become circular with open palms and the speech emphasis will be on having open and extending vowels. The planning is now centered on how that party will feel, and the feelings of all the guests. This plan will be very different from the plan motivated predominantly by thought. Again, once the teams have had a chance to plan, each team will share their ideas.

Finally, focusing on characters that are dominated by their will-force is the next party planning task. Now the movement can be more chaotic and even staccato, the speech is gruffer and guttural with more speed – "Gotta get things done!" The thumbs now dominate the gestures with palms closed – don't want to be vulnerable and expose any feelings! Characters may also dig in their heels as they want to be sure to get their way – they know best. Once this version of the party is planned the teams all share – and the commentary between teams might get a bit heated (all for theatrical fun of course), since each team will believe they know the way that party should happen.

Variation

Have trios or larger groups, each with differing predominant forces, improvise this party planning together to discover how the thinking, feeling, and will forces could all contribute and work in collaboration to create a successful event. A great improv to reflect life situations!

Improvisation 7: Solving the problem

The scenario is set up with a counselor meeting with a client. The counselor will decide if they are thinking, feeling, or will-force dominated and that is how they will approach the solving of their client's issue. The client also chooses their dominant force, and a problem they need solved by the counselor. This problem can be quite ridiculous as the point of the improvisation is to fully engage with these personality traits rather than the subject matter. The client should not pick a problem from their personal life but choose to be a character with a particular issue that would inspire them to seek assistance. Both characters should work to remain within their chosen area of feeling, thinking, or willing. These traits could also be given by a leader or peer rather than chosen. Once the improvisation proceeds, anyone viewing can call out freeze and go and replace the counselor, or the client, being sure they have already chosen whether they are a thinking, feeling, or willing character. This choice should be a different personality trait than what they observed from the first character, so if they were a feeling dominated character the new choice may be to approach the problem as a feeling character or a will-force dominated character. Freeze can be called out again so another participant can take the place of the counselor or client with the remaining trait, so all can witness how the approaches to the problem can be quite different depending on how the counselor approaches their client, and how the client approaches their problem. Should the issue be solved by one of the counselors, then the improvisation will begin again with new players.

Discussion/Reflection

What did you witness happening via the different personality traits and how the counselors approached the problem? Was the client able to remain with their dominant trait when a counselor changed? What happened when the client had a different dominant trait? If the problem was solved, how did the personality traits aid in the solution? Can you relate these traits to people you know or have observed in life?

Improvisation 8: The debate

Set up as a political debate might be, two characters will sit facing the group while a third acts as the moderator. A topic is chosen. Depending on your group, this could be a more relevant and important situation, such as climate change, or could be something humorous and silly, such as Coke vs. Pepsi. The actors then debate from their chosen point of view.

Discussion/Reflection

How did the personality traits influence the approaches to the topics? Did you observe traits that you have personally witnessed?

Group improvisation 9: Taking the psychological forces out to the museum (contributed by Paul Hurley, professional actor, Associate Professor of Acting and Movement at Kent State University, and certified teacher via NMCA)

This is an improv that I first learned in graduate school from my teacher Joann Browning. In this fun exercise, the performers explore taking on each of the psychological forces in a museum setting. Feel free to choose any kind of museum for this improv! For the following example I'll use an art museum. You can set up chairs, blocks, benches, etc. around the room to mockup imaginary paintings, sculptures, and installations. Once your space is created, you are ready to begin a playful exploration of each of the three psychological forces.

Below are some possible prompts to help guide the performers.

Thinking: Move about the museum operating from the THINKING Psychological Force. Explore moving in patterns and linear lines. Allow your head to be the leader. What kind of art are you drawn to? Who is the artist? What is the description of the painting (a THINKING individual might want to know the context for the painting)? What do you think of the artwork? Is it confusing and too abstract, or does it pique your curiosity? Maybe get up quite close to study each individual brushstroke of the artist. See the painting in all its specific detail. Perhaps you might need to consult the museum map for more information. When is the next tour? Is there a bathroom close by?

Feeling: Now move about the museum operating from the FEELING Psychological Force. Explore moving from your chest, playing around with more curving movements. What kind of artwork are you enjoying now? How do you feel about the painting, do you love it or hate it? Maybe you need to take a step back to fully take in the entire piece, allowing its beauty to wash over you. Perhaps you find yourself incredibly moved by the art around you.

Willing: Explore the museum operating from the WILL force. What section of the museum are you in? What kind of art are you drawn to? Or perhaps you're not interested in the art at all, and maybe are wondering if this museum has a restaurant or some snacks. Perhaps you are bored by the art, and you find yourself stretching or sprawling out on a bench, or maybe even annoyed that you were dragged to this museum in the first place. Explore asymmetrical postures and movements, allowing the pelvis and lower part of your body to take the lead.

Other variations

You can split the performers up into three groups, each group taking on either Thinking, Feeling, or Willing. This can be a lot of fun to play around with as the museum goers might interact with one another.

You can also experiment with having the group make quick changes between the centers. For an added layer of depth, you might invite folks to add one of the Qualities of Movement (molding, flowing, flying, or radiating) onto a Psychological Force, with variations like: a molding thinking force, a flowing feeling force, or a radiating will force. This can add wonderful texture and dimensions to the exercise!

Group improvisation 10: Becoming the artist (contributed by Paul Hurley)

One other follow-up improv you might explore is inviting the performers to become the artist creating the art utilizing each of the three psychological forces. What medium is each artist working within and with what materials? For example, the thinking artist might be very specific in each stroke of the brush, the feeling artist might paint from the heart in lavish grand brushstrokes, whereas the artist operating from the will force might be impulsively throwing paint against a large canvas or digging into some clay with their thumbs.

Wrap up

Explore the traits of thinking, feeling, and willing both in movement, dominant locations in the body, and speech. Improvising by isolating each trait will allow you to find unique behavior which can influence character creation, and how an objective is pursued.

Solo application

Observe these tendencies in the people around you, or even when interacting in the world with those you don't know but you may interact with for essential services. Imagine whether they are dominated by their thinking, feeling, or willing forces. When working alone, take on a task and accomplish it as if you are dominated by one of these traits, revealing how different the same task may be whether you are imagining yourself as a thinking, feeling, or willing character.

Script application

When you are analyzing a character you will be playing, ask yourself if they are predominantly driven by the forces of their thinking, feeling, or will. You can read through a script in the mindset of each one to determine this, or the character's stated behavior and reactions may make this clear to you. Play with using the accompanying movement and vocal traits for the character to make your rendition unique – moving in a linear way with precise speech as a thinking dominated character, in curves with extended vowels as a feeling character, and more sharply angled and deliberate in movement and speech as a will-force character. You may veil these quite a bit depending on the style of the production but allowing the resonance of psychology as influenced by these three areas will give you something solid to play.

Life application

When interacting with others, become aware of their tendency to approach situations from a thinking, feeling, or will-force point of view. This will allow you to compliment them by bringing in an alternate perception or looking with the same lens to better understand them. When determining solutions to your own situations, include seeing them from all these viewpoints to better determine the best and most balanced solution.

FIGURE 12.1 Five Actors looking in varied directions with a chair on the floor. Photograph by Melis Derya White. Actors L to R: Omar Moreno, Luis Alfonso Castro, Arleth Lopez, Shawn Pirkle, Aslan Longoria

12
ATMOSPHERES

"[A]tmospheres are limitless and to be found everywhere. Every landscape, every street, house, room; a library, a hospital, a cathedral, a noisy restaurant, a museum; morning, noon, twilight, night; spring, summer, fall, winter – every phenomenon and event has its own particular atmospheres".

"[W]e must make a clear distinction between the individual feelings of the characters and the atmospheres of the scenes. An atheist can maintain his skeptical feelings in an atmosphere of religious awe, or a man in grief can still carry his sorrow in his soul when entering an atmosphere of gaiety and happiness".

Michael Chekhov, To the Actor, *Routledge Press, revised, 2002, courtesy of the Michael Chekhov Estate*

The technique of employing atmospheres in a production is one that Michael Chekhov believed was often missing from performances but that it could be a powerful element that profoundly affects an audience. Think about your choices for a vacation. Some will choose to be in the atmosphere of a beach, with the crashing waves and sparkling sand, while others would have no interest in having sand between their toes and would opt for a bustling urban environment of concrete and steel. If you think about it, we are consistently making choices based on atmospheres. There are most likely restaurants that you choose to patronize because of their atmospheres, whether that be the loud comradery you enjoy in a bar lounge, or the quiet, romantic candle-lit ambience of a dining room. Entertainment has its own atmosphere, and you make choices based on what you enjoy experiencing – do you enjoy the excitement of a movie filled with action and suspense or the fun antics of a romantic comedy? While we may not always remember precise details of an event, we often remember the atmosphere we experienced, ranging from the joyous wedding to the somber funeral. You can now realize how important atmospheres are and how performers can influence an audience by creating an atmosphere for those audience members to experience.

Improvisation 1: Overall atmospheres

You can guide yourself through this exercise or if in a group everyone is guided to experience each atmosphere for themselves. First go to the periphery of the space you are in. Imagine that there is a threshold in front of you, and that beyond that threshold is a space that you can fill with whatever atmosphere you can imagine. To begin, you'll start with a place that has a certain atmosphere and that would be a cemetery at midnight. While you may have never been in a cemetery at midnight, your imagination can certainly fill in an atmosphere from what you have experienced and what you may have observed – or perhaps you make it up completely – it's all perfect. Imagine that the atmosphere of a cemetery at midnight exists up above you, in the collective consciousness of us all, and inhale that from above and as you exhale blow that atmosphere over the threshold and into the space that lies before you. Feel free to do this several times so that you truly feel you have imbued the space with that atmosphere of a cemetery at midnight. Once your imagination is convinced the atmosphere is there, take your hand across that imaginary line of the threshold into the space in front of you. Let just your hand experience that cemetery at midnight. Pull your hand back. Now just dip your toe into that atmosphere and be aware of how that atmosphere is affecting you. Take your toe back out. Now it's time to fully cross over that threshold and begin to walk through this atmosphere. Imagine the very air that surrounds you and that you are breathing is filled with this atmosphere of a cemetery at midnight. Once you've started moving in the space, imagine that you have thick dust on your shoes and brush that dust off. Be aware of how you are moving and achieving this task within the atmosphere. Where does your eye focus go as you bend down to brush off the dust? Is it only on the shoe or are you aware of the space around you? Do you notice any changes in your breathing? Once you have taken in this atmosphere, travel back to the periphery of the room, crossing that imaginary threshold. Once there, reach out and imagine packing that atmosphere into a compact ball and tossing that ball back up and out to the universe. It'll be there whenever you need it again.

Now that you have experienced the atmosphere of a place, you'll now work with the atmosphere of an event. The event does occur in a place, but it's really the event itself that most influences the atmosphere and for this improvisation the choice is a joy-filled wedding. This may be an event that you are quite familiar with or perhaps you've not attended a wedding – but have probably seen them in a film or TV program. Even if you haven't, know that the atmosphere of a joy-filled wedding exists out in the collective unconscious, and once again inhale that atmosphere from up above and exhale it into that space before you – across your threshold. Do this as many times as you need until you feel that atmosphere exists in front of you, just beyond the threshold. Once again, place just your hand across the threshold to experience the atmosphere. Be aware of any sensation in your hand – does it want to move? Then pull your hand back. Now dip your toes into that atmosphere. How do your toes react – how might they want to move? Bring your toes back and then bring your entire self into the atmosphere. Imagine molecules of joyous wedding are all around you and that you are breathing in those molecules, and they are penetrating your skin. You are absorbing this atmosphere and you begin moving within it. Images may come to you of specific wedding details, or you may just be moving within the atmosphere of a joyous wedding. After all, a joyous wedding could take place in a grand cathedral or in a modest backyard. The location is not the main element here but instead the event.

Discussion/Reflection

What sensations did you experience when you put in your hand or dipped your toe into the atmosphere? Were you able to sense the atmosphere around you by engaging your imagination? How did being in the atmosphere change you and your behavior? How did your specific sensations or feelings change depending on the atmosphere? Were you able to 'be' in the atmosphere rather than acting out the atmosphere?

Improvisation 2: Limitless imagery

Now it's time to create an atmosphere that is based on imagery alone. It's not a specific place or event but is simply an image that inspires your imagination. The late Mala Powers often used an atmosphere of champagne bubbles. Try this one and see what happens in the space for you if you imagine that all around you in the molecules of the air is the essence of champagne bubbles. Perhaps you catch the "bubbliness" of that atmosphere – perhaps you move through the space with a bit of a tipsy quality because that is how the champagne bubbles inspire you. Remember, you are not acting out champagne bubbles. Instead, the bubbles are in the air all around you and move through them and are acted upon by the molecules of that atmosphere. That influence then allows you to behave however you are inspired to by being immersed in that atmosphere. You may once again perform a simple action and be aware of how that action is influenced by the atmosphere.

Continue exploring a variety of images that are meaningful for you. It's helpful to utilize an adjective with the atmosphere to evoke more specific images. Perhaps you choose to work with an atmosphere of fire. What kind of fire is in that atmosphere? It could be a chaotic fire, or warm, cozy campfire, or uncontrolled blazing fire – all of which evoke very different images and would influence your behavior in different ways for each of those atmospheres. Perhaps you try an atmosphere of sticky cotton candy or vibrant pink feathers – go as far as your imagination can take you. If someone is leading this improvisation, they can provide the imagery for the group. We've probably all experienced or are aware of phrases such as, "the tension was so thick you could cut it with a knife". That phrase is indicative of a certain atmosphere and to be more concise for this exercise might simply be called "thick oppressive tension". The naming or baptizing, a word Michael Chekhov used, of the atmosphere, is important in order to create a strong image that all the players involved can immerse in.

Improvisation 3: Atmosphere orchestra

One half of the group will now be seated close together, facing each other. The other half of the group will be on the outside, with their backs to the inner circle. If there is a designated leader, they can provide an atmosphere to be created, or the inside circle could decide this as a group. The inside circle then creates an orchestra of sound, without words, to evoke the chosen atmosphere. This could be all sorts of noises with the voice or even movement such as tapping or clapping depending on what is right to create the given atmosphere. Those on the outside of this circle with their backs turned, simply let those sounds permeate them and allow any image of an atmosphere to exist. They may even start to move a bit within the atmosphere that they are receiving from the "orchestra". After a time, the orchestra ends, and those in the outside circle now turn in and are asked what atmosphere they received. As always, there is no right or wrong answer, but instead communicating what the imagination brought. After the inner circle has a chance to create several atmospheres with the outside circle responding, the teams switch.

Some ideas for these atmospheres are places such as: creepy haunted house, sinister carnival, tranquil tropical beach, or deep green forest. Ideas of event atmospheres are joyous wedding, disjointed job fair, somber funeral. Some ideas for imaginative atmospheres are sticky used gum, ebullient angelic song, or fluffy clouds.

Discussion/Reflection

Were you able to feel an atmosphere just by sound? Did any of the orchestra's atmospheres compel you to move in any certain way? As part of the orchestra, did you feel you were able to improvise as a unified ensemble to create the atmospheres?

Improvisation 4: Atmosphere molecules

Once again, one half of the group will convene in a close center circle while the other half is at a distance around them, with their back turned. A leader will then provide an atmosphere to be created by the inner group, or the group may decide as a team. Now, in addition to making sounds for the atmosphere, the inner circle adds movement and surrounds those in the outer circle. It is specified that there is no touching, but the inner circle can use other movements around their peers to create the atmosphere, imagining that they are molecules of whatever atmosphere was chosen. An atmosphere of enthusiastic fireflies might result in flicking hands and feet and flying about those in the outer circle. It's not necessary that the actual atmosphere being created is guessed, but rather the essence of that energy is conveyed.

As before, after each atmosphere is played for a time, it is dropped, and those in the outer circle will report what they received.

Discussion/Reflection

Was it easier to experience the atmosphere now that molecules of it were moving around you? Were those playing the molecules able to retain their focus? In reporting what you felt the atmosphere was, even if not the exact title, did you approximate what the essence of that atmosphere was?

Personal atmospheres

In addition to general, objective or overall atmospheres which we all experience together, or the atmospheres an ensemble of actors experience as they proceed through a production, there are personal atmospheres. These personal atmospheres are the essence that we carry with us always. They are not emotions, or moods, but instead how we operate within the world while having emotions or moods – our general persona. A simple example would be that some of us are generally optimists while others are pessimists. This typical way of being does not change based on activity or even isolated emotions, but instead is our overarching way of being in the world. Choosing a personal atmosphere for a character can help bring that character into a fuller existence and help to designate how that character will act in various situations. Each individual will bring their personal atmosphere into any overall or general atmosphere that exists and react in their own personalized way. A pessimist might attend a wedding and be rather sour during the event believing that the marriage will never last and citing statistics about the divorce rates. An optimist might be in that overall wedding atmosphere and be overwhelmed with joy for the newlywed couple, believing that love conquers all. For both it is the same overall atmosphere of a wedding, which may be further identified with specific adjectives such as opulent or down-home, but the way each individual plays within that atmosphere depends on their unique personality.

Improvisation 5: The birthday party (personal atmospheres)

For this improv, one half of the group (depending on size) will be guests at a birthday party and the rest will be observers. One performer is chosen as the host, it being their birthday, and the other guests will enter one at a time. Everyone participating will be given a particular personal atmosphere that they will explore as they enter the overall atmosphere of a birthday party. If there is a table and chairs and a few other props available to substitute as party platters or decorations, that will help keep the improv active. If there is a doorway that can be entered into the party space, the guests can be beyond the door and knock, with the host coming to let them in. If there isn't an accessible door or other entryway to use in that way, then an entrance can be established and mimed. In addition to being given the personal atmospheres, the presenters are also assigned a number. As the improv proceeds and all the guests have arrived and are interacting, the leader will call out a number. The performer with that corresponding number will then take focus and others give that person the focus. The action should not stop, or other performers freeze, but instead segue as smoothly as possible for that person to become the main focus. As different numbers are called, others take the focus so that everyone has an opportunity to have their moment, and have their behavior reveal clues as to their personal atmospheres. Once the improv has had time to develop, it is brought to a close and the viewers now get to guess what each person's personal atmosphere was, having the performance team stay in front for the discussion. Next those that are viewing will go onstage and repeat the improv while others become their audience.

Sample Personal Atmospheres: Optimist, Pessimist, Curiosity, Skepticism, Sensuosity, Paranoid, Narcissistic, Know-It-All, Analytical, Spacey, Confident, Argumentative, Naive – you can also add adjectives to make these even more specific and add the many more that you may have observed.

Discussion/Reflection

What traits did you see in each individual? Could you assign a particular personal atmosphere to these traits? How did everyone's atmosphere interact with the overall atmosphere of the birthday party? Did the overall atmosphere alter at times due to anyone's behavior? Did it become clearer how personal atmospheres can exist within an overall shared atmosphere? Did anyone's personal atmosphere start to influence or change the overall atmosphere? You will note that only one overall atmosphere can exist at any one time, and if a conflicting atmosphere begins, one will quickly or eventually become dominant.

Bonus atmosphere exercise: Thanksgiving stories (contributed by Anjalee Deshpande Hutchinson, Author, Interim Associate Provost for Equity and Inclusive Excellence and Professor of Theatre at Bucknell University, and certified teacher via NMCA; with very special thanks to super talented playwright and educator Stephanie Kyung Sun Walters, from whom many of these exercises are adapted)

In America, Thanksgiving is often painted as a joyous and warm celebration which brings family members together for a loving reunion. Yet this celebration (not unlike the holiday itself) is often deeply rooted in complex problematic pretenses, one of which the inability to acknowledge the holiday's roots in colonization, oppression, and genocide. How this deeply painful and often unacknowledged aspect of our shared history as Americans manifests in many American homes is in the revelation of individual family dysfunction. Like our cultural attempts at erasure and the unwillingness to acknowledge the historical massacres of indigenous peoples at the hands of our country's ancestors, individual families and family members often work hard to maintain a pleasant facade of kinship that does not reflect the truth of the relationships that often simmer just beneath the surface. How family members treat each other, hurt each other, disagree with each other, and blame each other for past transgressions begins and ends with a story. Family stories, secrets, and gossip shared during the holidays often reveal fraught relationships and reinforce problematic patterns. Stories can also unearth conflicting perceptions of events over the years.

The Thanksgiving Stories exercise is a series of writing improvisations that precede Michael Chekhov's atmosphere explorations for characters in plays that are in families together. These exercises deepen character development as well as the relationship between characters by discovering and cultivating shared "memories" in addition to individual imagery useful for application in a variety of ways including centers, backspace, psychological gesture, and many more Michael Chekhov tools for characterization.

To prepare for this exercise, have participants bring a notebook they like (or one their character would like) and a pen that writes easily. Also, they should have something comfortable to sit on such as a pillow or a folded blanket. Alternatively, you can also bring notebooks and many pens or markers as well as pillows and pitch them all over the room in cozy writing corners and nooks that can be used by any of the actors. Between each set of writing exercises and sharings, it is helpful to get actors on their feet and playing a game or another physical exercise to break up the energy of the room and keep it alive. The idea is to write for 5–10 minutes, to share for 10–15 minutes and to move every 20–25 minutes. Bonus if the participants find a new place in the room every time they sit down to write.

Introduction/warm up: Thanksgiving treats

Have students find their comfy writing spot and begin with a list of ten types of Thanksgiving foods. *If students don't or haven't celebrated Thanksgiving, ask them to think of a holiday in their family or culture that they would enjoy special foods. Example: in India where my family originates from, common family holidays that were often accompanied by traditional foods included Ganpati, Navratri, and Diwali. This list should be associated with the actor, not the character. Use a timer for three minutes. It is okay if they don't finish.

Once they complete their first list, have them complete a few more lists for practice. Each should be timed at three-minute intervals. Lists could include gross holiday foods, favorite holiday traditions, dreaded family conversation topics. These should all be related to the actors, not the characters.

Once participants have completed the lists, ask if anyone would like to share from any of the lists. They can read their whole list or just a few selections. Encourage them to share without contextualizing list items, just allow them to land as is. Do not force anyone to share but hopefully at least three to five people will share something interesting or amusing from their list. At the end of the sharing, make sure you point out a few things you found interesting or amusing from the sharings.

At the end of this writing section, have participants get up and play a game or another physical activity for 5–10 minutes and then return to a seated position anywhere in the room.

Transition to character: Family lists

Have students find their comfy writing spot and close their eyes. Perhaps lay down. Take a moment to have them relax with some deep breathing and centering, and then ask them to begin to draw down their character from the universal unconscious. Whatever shows up shows up, it doesn't need to be a complete understanding, whatever they know to begin is enough. Once they feel they have drawn down their character into their imagination and body, ask them to approach the next few writing prompts through the eyes and voice of their character.

Begin with a list of things that respond to the prompt: *Family is....* Make sure it is a list of multiple things, ideas, and images – no need to define or contextualize. Emphasize the ideas and images don't need to make sense to the actor, just whatever shows up. Use a timer for 3–5 minutes per list. It is okay if they don't finish. Other lists include *Family feels like.... Family looks like.... Family sounds like.... Family smells like...* etc. Once you complete three or four lists, ask if anyone would like to share. At the end of the sharing, make sure you point out a few things you found interesting from what students have shared.

At the end of this writing section, have participants get up and play a game or another physical activity for 5–10 minutes. If you choose, you can have them play the games as their character. At the end, have them return to a seated position anywhere in the room.

Collaborative writing: Three stories

Before the session begins, as the facilitator, create three or four index cards (or more for larger character families) and on each card write a one-line imagined core memory that *could have* happened between characters in the family in their past. The facilitator should feel free to take creative license on this imagined memory – nudging the characters in a way that will engage their imaginations but also stay within the given circumstances of the play.

Examples:

- The time I bought a Mother's Day present with my own allowance money but then <person X> ruined it on purpose.
- The time <person X> saw a bunch of bullies making fun of me at school and pretended they didn't know me.
- The time <person X = my parent> forgot me at school when I had to stay after.
- The time my family forgot my birthday.

Hand each participant one index card and on the card have them fill in the blanks with character names if you haven't already or cross out the "I's" and put their own character name. Then ask them to free-write in their notebook in the voice of their character chosen for this memory. Ask them not to worry about grammar or spelling or structure – just write whatever comes to mind. Ask them to be detailed in terms of images, smells, sights, and sounds as well as feelings. Give about five minutes or so for each memory.

Once you reach the time limit, have everyone stop, and then ask each actor to read their character memory out loud for everyone to hear. Once everyone has shared their story, have the actors pass their index cards to the next person in the circle. The next person in the circle will now spend 5 minutes writing about the incident (about the other people) written from their point of view. Tell actors not to change the event to make it about their character – rather imagine that your character remembers this same event happening to another character but ask how your character may remember it differently. You can use any details from the last round of sharing from other characters' "memories" which you can agree with, contradict, or interpret from the point of view of your character. Time this free-write for five minutes. Once you reach the time limit, have everyone stop, and then ask each actor to read their character memory out loud for everyone to hear.

Continue to pass each memory around and have each actor free-write in the voice of their character on this shared family memory from their character's point of view. Share at the end of each round.

Post-writing atmospheres

After the end of the Collaborative writing exercise, close with some atmosphere exercises. Consider family related atmospheres that begin with participants drawing down from the universal unconscious images from The Palace of / The World of / The Land of.... Family related atmospheres.
Examples:

- All I have inherited, What I wish I could forget, Memories I keep close to my heart, What I knew for sure, What I didn't know, What I wish she/he/they knew about me, What I frequently dream about, My recurring nightmare/s
- You can also craft the atmospheres to include words/images/phrases from the play script that you might want to include to get characters in the same physical world as well.

Conclusion

Once you have completed all the writing prompts, sharings and atmospheres, have participants close the session by returning to their notebooks to write down any relevant images and ideas that they may want to return to as they build their character moving forward. Feel free to end the session with sharing if there's time and interest. Hopefully your actors will have lots to work with and a shared base of memories on which to build which will influence their understanding of their own characters and well as their relationships with one another.

Wrap up

Experience a variety of atmospheres by using your imagination to immerse yourself in their essence. These can be places, events, or images. Consider a character's personal atmosphere – the essence that they carry with them into all atmospheres.

Solo application

As you travel to different spaces and events, be aware of the atmospheres that you experience and when alone recreate them through your imagination. Observe how those you encounter have their personal atmospheres and how those personal atmospheres influence their behavior. When alone and accomplishing basic tasks, play with taking on these personal atmospheres and note the change in how you act.

Script application

Consider your character's primary essence, their personal atmosphere, and note if that changes during their journey through the story. Oftentimes it is the circumstances that may change but not a character's essence. While the archetypal Cinderella undergoes a transformation from belittled stepdaughter to princess, and she experiences many mood swings as she encounters diverse general atmospheres – from the soot-ridden hearth at home to the opulence of the palace, her personal atmosphere stays the same. Another archetypal character, Ebenezer Scrooge, does have a change of personal atmosphere because of his journey through the various overall atmospheres of past and future, of parties and graveyards. The journey Scrooge takes inspires him to alter his personal essence from that of selfish greed to one of unbridled generosity. Noting all the changes in the overall atmospheres of a script allows you to bring those places and events alive for an audience and is much more doable and effective than trying to play individual traits of a space – such as the seeing of green leaves and the brown, rough bark of the imaginary trees, and smelling the crisp clean air and feeling the humidity on your skin and hearing the chirping of birds – all at once. If you take the time to create all of these in your imagination when they are called for, when it comes to perform there is much more to focus on. So, to be sure the atmosphere exists while you retain your character and pursue your objectives as that character, perhaps you baptize the above items as "Verdant Forest" which allows you to inspire all your senses to come alive via your imagination without the distraction of attempting to create items one at a time.

Life application

Be considerate by paying attention to atmospheres you enter and honoring the energy that is there, or, if appropriate, work to alter the atmosphere to a more positive one. Be aware that you can create atmosphere for others via the energy that you exude when in a certain space or when hosting an event. Understanding your own personal atmosphere will allow you to be aware of how you interact with others and tempering or expanding that personal atmosphere as necessary for a more positive outcome can be beneficial to you and those around you.

FIGURE 13.1 Three actors, one (center) clapping, two (beside) snapping. Photograph by Melis Derya White. Actors L to R: Luis Alfonso Castro, Arleth Lopez, Shawn Pirkle

13
TEMPO AND RHYTHM

> *"A small hint from a partner – a glance, a pause, a new or unexpected intonation, a movement, a sigh, or even a barely perceptible change of tempo – can become a creative impulse, and invitation to the other to improvise".*
>
> Michael Chekhov, To the Actor, *Routledge Press, revised, 2002, courtesy of the Michael Chekhov estate*

Actors, dancers, and musicians are all familiar with tempo and rhythm. It may have been a theatre director or choral instructor calling out: "pick up the pace" or a choir director banging out a rhythm to keep a group in sync. Michael Chekhov studied with widely known theatre practitioner Constantin Stanislavski, and tempo and rhythm were part of his technique. The teaching of NMCA goes beyond just pace and beat and incorporates five varied tempo/rhythms as well as actively experimenting with inner and outer tempo/rhythms, to develop the ability to create more complex characters.

Improvisation 1: Discovering tempo

For this exercise you will want to have as much space to move in as possible. If you are experimenting on your own, you may want to be in an open space outdoors or if working with a group an ideal setting would be a large open studio. For this exercise you want to envision a tempo scale of 1–10, with 1 being stillness and 10 as moving as fast as you can. As far as reaching 10, this may be walking at the fastest pace possible or breaking out into a run, depending on your spacing and your capabilities. The ultimate goal is to be safe – so adapt this accordingly! Particularly if you are working with a group all moving in a space simultaneously, you may want 10 to be the fastest walk possible with no running. Also, with a group you want to be sure everyone keeps their awareness high, and if you are heading into a collision to simply spin and head in another direction. Safety first!

Begin with 1, which corresponds to total stillness. Now, you may expect 0 to be stillness, but as a living being we are never truly still. Even when we freeze in space our heart continues to pump and our lungs expand and contract with breath, so 1 for me is most appropriate – there is still subtle movement, even if it is internal. Extend your awareness to all parts of the body to be sure a finger isn't twitching or a knee shaking. Aim for complete stillness which can be a powerful tool as a performer. Now, immediately move as fast as you can in the space without running, which will be labeled 10. You've now experienced both extremes of the scale, and let's find what is in between. Now starting back at 1, change to 2, which is as slow as you can go but still moving – you shouldn't be able to move any part of you very far! Then a 3 which is just a bit more, then up to 4 adding a bit more speed, and then building up to 5, your mid-point, which should be your typical speed when moving in a space. This may be your casual walk which gets you from one place to another. Then go up to 6, just a bit faster, and up to 7, 8, and 9, and finally work up to the fastest tempo of 10. Be sure to consider your level of comfort and ability and move at your own top speed – it's never a competition. However, you want to feel your energy as you move as fast as you possibly can. If working in a space with a group, the best way to keep everyone safe is that a 10 is the fastest walk everyone can do, prior to bursting into a run. Remember if you are heading directly toward someone to simply spin in another direction without losing your momentum – but still staying safe. In addition to working with this tempo scale, this is a great exercise in awareness – both of the self and of your environment and everyone in it. Once you have established this scale, begin to jump numbers so you develop the capacity to go from the stillness of 1 to instantly moving as fast as you can in a 10. This juxtaposition offers an excellent way to create exciting moments on stage, and these numbers give you a vocabulary. You could score your script with these numbers to designate the tempo of delivery for your performance, and a director can use these numbers for shorthand and ask an actor to "bring that tempo from a 5 up to an 8" or "slow that down from what seems to be a 7 all the way to a 3". The ability to technically change your tempo will also provide a variety of results for your audience.

The next round, continue to play with tempo but now add breath and voice. You will have much more breath control when still than at your top speed of 10, but if you stay with the various tempos your voice should change accordingly. Once you find the movement/voice connection you could later apply these tempos just to voice – speaking very slowly and deliberately at a 2, and then spitting out words when at a 10 – both of which may be appropriate for certain characters and situations that arise in performance. Beginning with the stillness of 1 and being aware of the breath, add speech even though this will require a bit of movement in order to articulate. The energy of someone standing perfectly still but also speaking can be quite compelling. Continue to work through the tempo scale, simply reciting numbers, letters, or some memorized lines if available, so you experience the full range of tempos that your voice now experiences as well as your body. Once you have married the body and the voice via tempo, "veil" the physicality of the tempo and practice the scale of 1–10 but now just with the voice. It's near impossible not to also move physically as you work your way up to 10 vocally, so sitting in a chair for the exercise might assist you in moving less while still building up the tempo of the voice. Once you complete this exercise you can then assign varying numbers for the body and voice. What happens if your body is in 1, stillness, but the voice is speaking at a tempo of 10. What if you are moving through space as quickly as you can at a 10, and your voice is being produced very slowly at a tempo of 2. These exercises allow you to develop tempo skills with your body and voice that will allow you excellent flexibility when playing characters and situations. The ideal with any technique is that it is not visible and disappears once in performance, but the groundwork needs to be laid.

Improvisation 2: Playing with rhythm (legato, staccato, waltz, pandemonium, stillness)

Five various rhythms will be introduced here, with the idea that with these basics any combination could be created. Michael Chekhov's work emphasizes two rhythms with the first being legato. In the Oxford Dictionary, legato is defined as "in a smooth flowing manner, without breaks between notes". You'll note that legato is most often referenced in music, but for this exercise you will apply legato to your physical movements, and then also to voice.

Legato

To begin, move in space with a smooth and flowing manner as indicated by the definition. Use large and open abstract movements so that you can experience your entire body moving in this way. Your arm can lift and reach with legato energy and be sure every step you take has smoothness and flow. Michael Chekhov referred to these exercises as "psycho-physical", so be sure to keep your awareness open to experience this movement via your mind and feelings as well as through your body. Once you feel successful moving in this legato fashion, check in with your breath, allowing it to smoothly flow in and out. As you exhale take a touch of sound, so you begin to connect the voice to your movement. Then let that touch of sound develop into speech, using letters, numbers, or some memorized text.

How does legato make you feel? What type of character might move in this manner? How was your vocal production similar or different from your typical way of speaking? What sort of feeling/energy might this convey to an audience?

Staccato

Now you want to move in a staccato manner. The Oxford Dictionary defines staccato as: "performed with each note sharply detached or separated from the others". Again, you will apply this typically musical term to the body – moving sharply and distinctly with movements that don't necessarily follow each other – random body parts can move rather than be sequential. Once you feel successful with this staccato movement, connect with your breath. Is the breath choppy now as the movement tends to be? Are you taking in more or less breath? Let a touch of sound occur as you exhale to get in touch with the sound connected to your staccato movement. Is it a different pitch than your typical voice? Build into reciting letters, numbers, or some memorized text to fully experience this staccato rhythm in both body and voice. Be sure to also be aware of how this feels to you.

How was this staccato movement similar/different from your movement in everyday life? Were there certain feelings or emotions that bubbled up via this movement? How did your breath and voice change? What do you think presenting staccato movement and voice might convey to an audience? What characters or situations might incorporate staccato movement?

Waltz

The next rhythm to experiment with is the waltz rhythm. This is an extension of the legato rhythm, but now it adds an elongation on the initial beat of three beats and is one of the simpler dance rhythms to experience. Liveabout.com/waltz explains on their site: "Waltz music is written in ¾ time, counted as '1,2,3/1,2,3'. The first beat of each measure is accented, corresponding to the extended, highly stretched step that is taken on the first count, followed by two short steps. With its distinctive rhythm pattern, the Waltz is easy to recognize and simple to learn".

This exercise is to apply the waltz rhythm to the body, not necessarily to dance, but to experience this universal rhythm of slow, quick, quick or elongation, and then two short beats and then back again to the accented first beat. Start to move in the space with this new rhythm, which is a combination rather than strictly one rhythm as legato and staccato were. No need to think about dancing but instead simply experience how it feels to elongate a beat and follow it with short beats. Once you have this rhythm established, let sound flow within this rhythm in order to connect with your voice, as you have done previously.

How did this feel to have the beat change as you moved? Did a character type emerge for you? Did certain feelings arise that you might associate with this way of moving?

Pandemonium

After experiencing the gentleness and distinct pattern of the waltz rhythm it's time to experience moving without any pattern whatsoever, but to instead move with a variety of tempos in all different directions. Let's call this movement pandemonium! From vocabulary.com: "Pandemonium is chaos, total and utter craziness". How fun is this to move with chaos and utter craziness! Using this as one of the psycho-physical exercises, allow yourself to fully commit to the pandemonium and experience where it brings you. This is moving with a lack of pattern – any which way at any tempo. As you move, connect with your breath, then touches of sound, and then, as before, take it into speech to discover how your voice reacts to this pandemonium.

How did moving with pandemonium make you feel? When might a character experience this sort of energy pattern? What happened to your speech when you spoke from this energy? When might a character vocally express themselves this way? What might this type of energy convey to an audience?

Stillness

The fifth and final "rhythm" is back to stillness as explored in tempo. Stillness has its own rhythm, particularly when in stillness you pay attention to what your body is doing – from your pulse to your breath. With stillness added to the above rhythms, you can create a variety of interesting patterns – breaking from stillness into pandemonium or into staccato.... or moving along in a waltz rhythm to a sudden stop. It's often these moments of stillness that can create intrigue within a performance.

Improvisation 3: Rhythm in music

An article in Backstage.com bears the title: "How Music Can Help You Develop a Character". The article suggests you may create a playlist of what your character might listen to, or even develop a theme song for your character that inspires your interpretation of the character. For this exercise, the leader will assemble a variety of musical clips to play for the group. The participants will move to the music in any way that they are inspired to move, given the tempo and rhythm of the music being played. Akin to musical chairs, the leader will abruptly stop the music. The movement can now subside or become veiled, as participants now engage in conversation inspired by the tempo/rhythm they just experienced. This is pure improvisation so be sure to subscribe to the "yes and" model of interaction and see what happens. Once various "characters" have had a chance to establish conversations with each other, the leader will call out "Freeze" and then one team at a time will be "unfrozen" so others can hear their discussion and view the characters that came because of the musical springboard. Suggestions of musical genres include pop, rock, gospel, heavy metal, blues, jazz, classical, musical theatre up-tempo, musical theatre ballad, hymns, country western, hip-hop, rap… the choices are endless!

Improvisation 4: It's all in your head

Now that participants have moved and improvised to actual music, it's time to employ the imagination, and work in a way that is more akin to what may happen in a performance. For a performance, an actor may choose to have music playing inside their head as subtext or a theme for the character that affects the way they move and speak. There would not be any actual music playing, but the influence of imagined music and the tempo/rhythm they create can contribute to characterization. Like the above, the leader will now call out genres of music, but not actually play anything. Participants will once again move to the imagined music, and most likely will create a specific song in their head that inspires them. It may be that they aren't familiar with a genre of music that is called and that is "perfect" – they let their imagination respond to the cue given and simply move with it. After a short time, the leader will call out "Go!", which is the cue for participants to now interact with each other with whatever characters emerge from the genre of music that was given. Again, this is pure improvisation, and there are no predetermined topics – go wherever your imagination decides to take you and be sure to accept what others give you and continue to create from those impulses and ideas. Once again, the leader can call out freeze after conversations are established, and then unfreeze one team at a time so others can view what's happened.

Discussion/Reflection

How did the genres of music influence your movement? Your voice and speech? Did characters easily emerge from the springboard of music both heard and then imagined? Was it easier to create from the imagined music having improvised with actual music initially? What types of characters did you interact with? Were you able to remain active in the improvisation by always thinking "Yes, and…" and flowing with what was given to you in the moment and adding to it? Did any specific feelings/attitudes arise from the various musical genres? Can you envision using music as part of your characterization for a performance?

Improvisation 5: Duos with audience

For this improv, the leader will provide a table of assorted props. Two volunteers will come to the table, in front of the remaining group who becomes the audience. The duo in front is now cast as detectives, and their task is to investigate these items and determine how they were used in a recent robbery and how they may lead to finding the suspects. Rather than employing the typical rule of "Yes, and…" of improv, where you accept your acting partner's offering and move forward, this scenario may lead more to "Maybe, and perhaps…", as the detectives share their hypotheses about the items in their effort to solve the case. Given the plethora of detective-based television shows and movies, this should be an enjoyable scenario for the participants to create and to view.

Version 1

After the scene begins, the leader now calls out numbers corresponding to tempo, and the actors utilize that number and continue the scene. Calling out a 1, stillness, may lead to the audience viewing two detectives who have paused for deep reflection about this case. A 10, the fastest tempo, may result in viewing detectives who are desperate as perhaps this case must be solved before the suspects have time to escape.

Version 2

Rather than tempos, now the leader will choose one of the five rhythms experienced previously when exercising these tools. When the detectives work in a legato rhythm, it may appear that they are remaining completely calm about this whole case, which could result in them seeming uninterested or completely confident, depending on how they use the rhythm. Moving with pandemonium may reveal ineptitude or their dedication to urgency. As with the previous performance tools, there is no negative or positive attribute to any of the tempos or rhythms and instead the results will be determined via the qualities that the actors add to these tasks.

Version 3

Combining tempo and rhythm, the leader could either play a quick snippet of music from a particular genre and the detectives now incorporate that into the scene, or the leader could simply call out a genre and the actors implement it via their imagination. This will no doubt result in some very humorous renditions of detective work as they may work in a "heavy metal" way or a Broadway up-tempo way to solve this crime.

Improvisation 6: Chekhov square dance! (contributed by Josh Chenard, Actor, Director, Visiting Professor at Colorado State University, certified teacher via the NMCA)

A fun physical and ensemble-based activity to present any group late in their Michael Chekhov training, the Chekhov Square Dance explores tempo and rhythm while reviewing previous Chekhovian concepts and elements. Rooted in traditional square dance sound and style, the design of this activity remains open and flexible.

Larger groups should be broken into two lines of course/workshop participants facing one another and smaller groups into a circle. In either case, after the activity is called, everyone moves to the center, performs the specific activity, then crosses to the opposite side of the space or circle.

It is up to the instructor and the group whether physical interactions occur in the center of the space during the dance such as linking arms, clapping hands, or connecting palm to palm and moving in a circle dosey-do style!

Typically, the course or workshop instructor serves as the caller, and music infuses the activity with an authentic square dance atmosphere. I always use Tommy Jackson/s Square Dance without Calls from 1959 which is easily found on YouTube.

Once everyone is lined (or circled) up and ready to dance, start the music, encourage clapping, and enjoy the fun! I give as many beats as needed between the calls for participants to perform the task and end on the opposite side of where they began. The ten calls below are what I use, but feel free to change, add, or alter anything based on your curriculum.

Chekhov Square Dance Calls:

- Let's start this dance, I'll even ask please, cross the room with a sense of EASE!
- Listen up now, do as you're told, when you cross your partner, slow down to a MOLD!
- One more quality, let's give it a try, spread those arms, let's see you FLY!
- Here we go, this makes me grin, move across that floor, leading with a bouncy CHIN!
- One more shift, from point A to B, move your center from chin to droopy KNEE!
- More fun from Chekhov Land, when you get to center, pause, and EXPAND!
- Archetypal Gestures are an acting gift, stop halfway, give me a LIFT!
- One more gesture, watch out – don't crash, one side to the other, stop and SMASH!
- Crossing again, move like on a boat, add some legato, let's see you FLOAT!
- Final cross, grow big and defiant, your IMAGINARY BODY is the Jolly Green Giant!

Wrap up

Work in various ways with the many tempos and rhythms that you can imagine to find endless variety in your performances. Make choices as to the tempo of a character's movement and discover if they have a certain rhythm. Then try it another way!

Solo application

In your "homeplay" you can have fun trying dialogue at varying tempos or exploring rhythm applied to the dialogue. You can apply these to simple actions such as preparing a meal, noting how the energy and feelings change depending upon what tempo and rhythm you may have chosen. Play a variety of music and move to the beat, trying some actions that a character may have. Continue to discover the endless ways that tempo and rhythm can affect you and be utilized for characterization and to enhance specific genres of performance.

Script application

Tempo and rhythm may apply to your specific character, the genre and atmosphere of the particular text, and/or how actions are pursued. Examine the text for clues and play with a variety of tempos to see if a fast pace brings the work to life or if a slower pace really allows the words to land, or a combination that allows for ideas to be fully emphasized. You may discover your character has a particular rhythm which could be the way they lift their arm each time or how they end a sentence or in their walk. Of course, in performing Shakespeare, the text in iambic pentameter will provide you with rhythm, and that deliberate rhythm holds incredible clues as to the meaning and actions being taken. Finding similar clues in more contemporary work will come from your experimentation and from trusting your imagination and instinct to guide you with tempo and rhythm.

Life application

Being acquainted with tempo and how you can change it and the way it influences you could be quite beneficial in life. You may be operating at a very quick tempo which could cause stress, and then could will yourself to bring that tempo down to a manageable 5 so that you are more careful with your tasks. There may have been an event which you responded to with pandemonium and deciding to alter that to a legato rhythm may make dealing with the situation much more manageable and allow you to remain calm in the face of adversity. In contrast, perhaps you want to bring pandemonium to the dance floor at a wedding, to get your friends energized and moving with an unbounded sense of fun!

FIGURE 14.1 Four actors standing, one sitting in front, looking various places. Photograph by Melis Derya White. Actors L to R: Luis Alfonso Castro, Omar Moreno, Arleth Lopez, Aslan Longoria, Shawn Pirkle

14
Focal Points

"How one decides where to focus, whether this decision is for the character or the self, is to identify the objective. When one is clear on the aim and purpose one is pursuing, the choice of where to focus becomes clearer".

Lisa Loving Dalton, Co-Founder, and
President of NMCA

Most performers are probably familiar with a well-known technique, typically attributed to Constantin Stanislavski as the creator, called circles of concentration. With this technique the performer begins by concentrating just in the vicinity close to the body – perhaps looking down at their hands or something within inches of their eyes. Then, as if imagining a spotlight that becomes larger, they begin to take in more of the space…perhaps at first a foot from the body, then a larger area, and if onstage, eventually the entire stage, and then out into the audience. This exercise can be very helpful in calming stage fright, to at first simply be in your own small world and then slowly expand that world to include all that is around you. Some stage actors talk about blocking out the audience to feel comfortable, but a stage performance is an interaction with the audience. In a comedy, you need to take in the audience to know when to pause for a laugh, or when to continue when an expected laugh doesn't come. Other performers talk about the energy that they receive from the audience, and how that helps propel them through the production. Whether you are ignoring the audience or deliberately allowing the audience in, their energy is palpable and should be recognized and appreciated. Not only onstage, but those that may surround you on a film or tv project are your "live" audience and can provide you with a similar energy.

As an individual actor, you want to be aware of your own energy onstage, and where you focus that energy. The five focal points, as adapted by NMCA, allow you to more naturally experience where your focus goes, which happens organically in life situations. As a performer, you want to have the ability to choose where your focus goes to create the effects that best serve the story you are depicting. Working with these focal points also will allow you to be much more flexible when a director asks for you to behave in a way that you hadn't considered for any given character. Considering where your focal point might be as a result of a given direction could be the key to the character's behavior that informs the audience of their state of mind – and how they are relating to the others in a scene.

Improvisation 1: Discovering the five focal points
Focal point #1 (FP1)

Sitting or standing, begin with FP1, which is for you to look directly at yourself. Rather than concentrating on an area as mentioned before, you are now focused on where your eyes are focused. For FP1, this is directly on you. You might be looking at your fingernail and seeing how the color has chipped. Perhaps you see a piece of lint on your shirt which you then brush off. Continue to focus on your entire self, what you can see of yourself, from your toes all the way up the body. Can you look to the side and see your own shoulder? The more ways you can experiment with looking at yourself the more choices you will have for future characters.

Focal point #2 (FP2)

If you are working with others this is the time to incorporate them into the exercise. Focus in FP2 is on the other, making direct eye contact with the person or people near you. This type of focus is how actors just beginning their training can have a technique which allows them to make direct eye contact with their partner without the discomfort that can sometimes occur. After all, it's an exercise! Later incorporating all of these focal points will give choices that can alleviate another trait sometimes seen in beginning actors – consistently remaining in FP2 and staring at their scene partner. If you watch conversations in life, this non-stop staring is not realistic. We all look in other directions for various reasons, and the focal points allow us to understand those reasons.

Focal point #3 (FP3)

This is the environment. Truly look at everything that is surrounding you. The space itself, items in the space, colors, textures, truly seeing all the details. An instructor can give this instruction and then clap, asking that on the clap everyone call out at once what they just noticed and then continue. This idea works well with a group milling about the environment and really looking at everything they pass by. It's a great way to begin a class as it can get a group to truly be in the present moment. You can include the people that are passing by as part of the environment – not making eye contact but instead noticing items of clothing, glasses, watches, or t-shirt slogans. This is an excellent exercise to increase your powers of observation and to be specific with detail.

Focal point #4 (FP4)

This may seem a bit more abstract but once you try it and recognize what it is then you will realize you go to this focal point often. This is a focus within your mind, but is very specific, such as thinking about what you need to do later in the day, or what happened last night. Maybe you are making a list in your head of what you need to buy at the store later. It is a very specific place within your mind and therefore takes some concentration to stay there. Theatrical monologues are often memories, and an actor may be tempted to stay within this FP4 the entire time, recollecting the event, but that would result in a one-level performance. Using these other focal points will remind the actor that their character is telling someone their story for a reason, they have an objective/intention, so FP2 with direct eye contact may come into play, or perhaps they reach an embarrassing point and go into FP1, or something in the environment distracts them and they head to focal FP3. As always, there is no right or wrong, only artistic choices that can lead to a multi-leveled performance.

Focal point #5 (FP5)

You might say that this focal point is everywhere and nowhere at the same time. I experience it as a cosmic pause, where there is no defined thought and perhaps your jaw even drops open with a "duh" expression. We all have experienced this…those moments where we simply "space out" and nothing is going on…or perhaps everything is going on. Typically, there would be no speech during one of these moments, but for the sake of interacting, when improvising, speech could come even when working with this focal point. However, if you remain true to the focal point and maintain that feeling of being out in space, some very strange interactions can occur.

Improvisation 2: Ball catch with focal points

Focal point #1

Each member of the group should have access to a ball, ideally one that is soft and squishy so that if anyone accidentally is hit they will remain unharmed. To begin, FP1 is used – the self. The ball now becomes an accessory that is moved around the body while the focus remains on the physical body of each participant. The participant wants to be sure that the ball is simply moving – perhaps from hand to hand or rolling down the arm or wherever it might go while the focus is on the self. This develops the capacity to work with a prop which is part of the environment, within FP3, but still able to remain in FP1.

Focal point #2

Now the focus is on "the other" – your peer participants. You can begin with just one ball being in play, and everyone is focused on who has the ball, and that person then makes eye contact and throws the ball directly to someone else. Again, while the ball is part of the environment, the focal point remains on the other players, so that the ball is simply a means to keep in contact with one another. This can also remind everyone of each other's names, as you may choose to call out the name of the person you are sending to, or if you are still learning names, your own name, and later you may simply send the ball silently. Not looking at the ball but instead maintaining eye contact means the ball may travel in a surprising way, but it's all perfect. The aim is to remain in FP2.

Focal point #3

Everyone goes back to working with their own individual balls, now tossing them up in the air and focusing on the balls as part of the environment around them, and the space into which the balls travel. No heed is given directly to what others are doing but instead the focus is on truly seeing the environment, which may include others, but without direct contact. If others are in the trajectory of the individual ball, they are part of the surroundings. You may toss the ball into the environment as you connect with everything around you, and perhaps your ball now becomes part of someone else's environment for a moment until you retrieve it.

Focal point #4

The ball continues to be tossed by each individual, but now it becomes a prop that almost unconsciously moves as each participant thinks about something very specific within their mind. The toss of the ball should be an afterthought or a way to remain focused on your thoughts. Pick something specific – an activity you need to do in the future, or a specific memory. Remain focused on all of the details of that activity while the ball stays in motion. Surely, we have all unconsciously chewed a fingernail or tapped a pencil – and observed such actions – while the mind was focused elsewhere. This is an excellent way to work with a prop in a naturalistic way while remaining focused on a specific thought in the mind.

Focal point #5

This focal point can be called nowhere, everywhere or the "duh" moment – the times we have when we simply space out. Perhaps we go away to an unknown place or exist everywhere at once and these moments are typically quite short – or hopefully are! For this, each individual will go into that spaced out place while also moving the ball. There's no need to be looking at the ball and in fact the eyes should momentarily lose their focus – they gloss over and may seem to stare into nothingness.

However, the ball becomes a prop that relays this state of being, as it is unconsciously moved while remaining in this focal point. This may be an all-too-often state for a comical character, or allow for a poignant pause within a drama.

Improvisation 3: Ball toss chaos

The activity above continues, beginning with each participant picking a focal point that allows them to work with their individual ball. This could go back to moving it on the body, or tossing it into the environment, thinking a specific thought, or spacing out for a moment. However, at any moment, anyone can call someone's name and then their focus immediately goes to FP2, the focus on the other, and both now must be in FP2. This might continue for a while, tossing back and forth between two individuals, or other names are called, and they begin to join in FP2. At any point, someone can choose to drop into another focal point and pick up their own ball. This prompts everyone to be directly engaged in the moment as you don't know when your name will be called, and you must leave the focal point you were in and give the attention to your peer, instantly going into FP2.

Improvisation 4: Inner monologue of focal points

Now that the focal points have been established, a leader can conduct participants to walk randomly in the space, and to allow a stream of consciousness to inspire speech. It may begin with literally speaking, "I'm walking around this space. I'm putting one foot in front of the other. My arms are swinging". The stream of consciousness is to note the literal experience. The leader then begins to call out focal points, "FP1 – you!" It's best that everyone pauses in the space and stays in one location here, so there aren't any crashes. Now each actor looks at themselves and continues speaking with what they are experiencing, which may be: "I'm looking at my shirt. I see wrinkles. I like this color blue". Now the temptation may be to go into another focal point, such as FP4 with, "I should have ironed my shirt. Where is my iron anyway? I think it's up on the shelf in the closet". This is a terrific moment to be conscious of and shows how we all go from one focal point to another with ease. With this improvisation however, the purpose is to solely utilize one focal point at a time to learn how you experience each one. Next, the leader conducts the participants to roam the room and calls out, "FP2 – them" once again. Now everyone focuses on making direct eye contact with the person they pass...perhaps holding for a moment, or simply moving on to the next person – however it occurs for each individual. What a terrific exercise for a group that is just getting to know one another, and perhaps direct eye contact is awkward at this point in time. However, being conducted to make that eye contact can take away any feeling of discomfort as you are simply following directions. A younger class may get a bit "goofy" with this one, but that's ok. Allow the giggles and laughter to play out as everyone connects with one another. For this focal point, the stream of conscious speaking may simply be, "I see you". Once everyone appears to have connected with all the individuals in the group, the leader can call out, "FP3 – the environment". The speaking should now specifically relate to everything that is viewed in the space. "There is a vent. The walls are green. The ceiling is made up of panels". Again, if the thoughts wander to, "I wonder why there are panels on the ceiling and not sheetrock. Maybe there are pipes under the panels and access is needed to them". This would then become a specific thought within the mind and be FP4. Again, to note this is an excellent way to recognize the distinction of the focal points. Next the leader will call out, "FP4 – a specific place with your mind. You are in your own head now". This may result in some participants stopping to really think their thoughts or they may continue walking. Some of us know that pacing allows us to think through situations and that may be a very familiar pattern – to walk and think simultaneously. This is simply an individual choice, but later more thought could be given to a character's way of accessing thought – in stillness or in motion. Now the stream of consciousness speaking may go anywhere and will be personal to each individual. It may be that very low voices and whispering happens, as individuals may feel vulnerable sharing their thoughts, and that is perfect.

Next the leader will call out, "FP5 – everywhere and nowhere...a duh moment". Again, this may result in most individuals stopping as they "space out" for a moment, not even being able to control their motor skills. Some may continue moving but the tempo may slow way down.

There's no need to stay FP5 for very long as when it happens in life, it is typically momentary – or hopefully is! No judgment – we all have our moments!

Improvisation 5

While this is fun to watch individual duos, and it can be very revealing for the audience to learn by observation, you could also choose to have everyone working at the same time, or split into two groups – whatever is best for your situation.

> Who: Siblings, a couple, best friends – you can alter these and also base them on the individuals participating
> Where: A Flea Market
> What: A table with items (ideally the leader puts out numerous props)
> Objective: Each character desperately wants every item on the table, so there will need to be a negotiation as to who will buy which item

Improvisation 6: Audience input

This improvisation uses "calling", meaning people outside of the scene act as side coaches for each character and call out the focal points at random times as the scene progresses. One person is assigned to each character, so that there are two distinct voices calling out the focal points. It also helps if the callers are on opposite sides of the audience or viewing area. If everyone is working on this improvisation in varied parts of the space at the same time, then groups of four will be ideal. Two act the scene and the two others are callers. The results will be a multi-leveled relationship which alters drastically depending on which focal point characters are in at any given time. This improv can be repeated many times, as the results will always vary depending on the focal points being called. Once a group becomes more familiar with the focal points, the callers may choose to act as directors, calling focal points purposefully to change the direction of the scene. This demonstrates how the story and relationship change, based solely on this one technique of focal points.

The situation from the fifth improvisation can be used, and more ideas are below. Working with objects is always helpful to keep the action flowing and provides easy access to FP3 – parts of the environment.

Additional scenarios to improvise

Two fashion designers choosing clothing items to dress a celebrity for an award show, but both have their own ideas for a look and will have to come to a compromise

Siblings in their grandparent's attic and now that they are gone, they are both feeling nostalgic and want everything in sight – the negotiation begins

Improvisation 7: Focal point moments – Enriching the Passing Moments of a Role (contributed by Professor Baron Kelly, University of Wisconsin – Madison, Department of Theatre & Drama and Division of Continuing Studies)

The actor should experience no moment of any role without some personal experience caused for the character. Actors learn to work using focal points in the creative process to create texture and levels in playing a role. All actors should consider focal points part of any scenic reality. So many seemingly unconscious activities can inspire the actor to enrich the passing moments of a role by allowing all sorts of associations to arise. The actor can express anything they feel in any way that an impulse suggests to them. Focal points can be very productive for an actor.

There is no moment in life when all three or at least two focal points are not hovering at the edge of the actor's concentration, tugging for their attention. The actor must remember that "this moment" is not the only "this moment" for the character.

Personal experience focal point

Some actors make the mistake of totally and continually isolating themselves from other characters and situations around them. In doing that, they miss the "pull" of conditions that intrude upon their concentration. A character can participate in a situation while looking at their character's problem and encourage the body responses generated by that personal experience rather than by the situation or the other person(s) involved.

Immediate Situation Focal Point

When an actor concentrates only on the personal experience such as the Immediate Situation during a beat, the situation is often all the actor sees, no matter where the actor looks. The actor's character feels that the problem of the situation is coming at them from all directions.

Outside the Immediate Situation Focal Point

Outside the Immediate Situation can suggest any number of things for the actor. Using Outside the Immediate Situation as a focal point, the moment of what will happen in tomorrow, yesterday, or later in a character's life can present many unconscious human activities to enrich the passing moments of a role.

Situation

A restaurant worker talking with their roommate after coming home from work at night, probably has tired feet, takes off their shoes, and rubs them (Personal Experience Focal Point); has a tired body (Personal Experience Focal Point) that needs to have clothing loosed to relax; has a backache (Immediate Situation Focal Point); has a headache from the noisy restaurant (Immediate Situation/ Outside Immediate Situation Focal Point); irritation at being held up in a traffic jam (Outside Immediate Situation Focal Point); cleaning eyeglasses (Immediate Situation Focal Point).

The worker might have cash tips received from a good work shift (Outside Immediate Situation Focal Point) and not yet had time for them to be counted (Outside Immediate Situation Focal Point); might find a spot from spilling something (Outside/Immediate Situation Focal Point) on their pants; Their shirt feels sticky to the body from sweating at work (Outside Immediate Situation Focal Point).

Using focal points allows actors to think in and as the character. The actors will discover how using focal points affects the playing of their actions and objectives. Play the improvisation many times, allowing whatever imaginative associations to arise while concentrating on the different focal points. Don't indulge in the focal point and neglect the objective of the scene.

Wrap up

Using focal points in various improvisations allows the performer to become more familiar with a natural way to vary the gaze, creating a more believable performance for an audience. Trying various locations of focus can also lead to more unique interpretations of a text, and provide a way to communicate subtext.

Solo application

Observe others in life and watch the way their focus points change in any given conversation. This can be especially fun as a casual observer in a crowded location such as a food court. The observations you make will allow you to realize that the gaze does indeed go to different areas and does not just stay glued upon the eyes of someone's companion. When working on a monologue, make it part of your "homeplay" to alter your focal points and then examine how the differences can create nuances in your presentation.

Script application

As you examine your script, think about the behavior of your character and where their focus might be at any one time. Are you always making direct eye contact with your scene partner(s)? That is not typical for anyone in life, so playing with changes in focal points can result in a more realistic portrayal of a character. You do want to consider your reaction when your scene partner is making direct eye contact with you. Do you face them directly? Are you uncomfortable and may shift into FP1, with self-focus due to you feeling self-conscious? Maybe you are distracted for a moment by something in the environment so switch to FP3 and then maybe you go back to FP2 with direct eye contact, but then want to relay a specific moment and you go to FP4 and then maybe you have a moment where you get lost and touch on FP5. You need to be in connection with your scene partner to realize how all of these may work for you and how the character may react. The focal points can be especially helpful when preparing a monologue for an audition or presentation, as even when acting solo, you can find terrific variety by applying these. When are you in direct contact with your imagined partner, and why and when might those focal points change?

Life application

By working with these focal points, you will become aware of your own habits, and where it is you tend to focus, as well as when and why. Perhaps it will benefit you to be more in FP2 with whomever you are talking to so that you make a stronger connection. Perhaps going into FP4, that specific thought in your head, will allow you to remember something more easily. Using FP3 can help you become aware of your environment and may even lead to you moving through space more safely. Perhaps realizing when you've gone into FP5 will allow you to snap back more quickly to the task at hand. Knowing that we all use these various focal points will allow you to be more accepting and understanding of those that may not be as comfortable with certain focal points, such as averting their eyes away from FP2, which may simply be shyness. Working within the focal points others have chosen can allow us to connect more effectively and in an accepting way.

FIGURE 15.1 Two actors with arms up in triumph, three actors crouching down. Photograph by Melis Derya White. Actors L to R: Aslan Longoria, Luis Alfonso Castro, Omar Moreno, Arleth Lopez, Shawn Pirkle

15
PSYCHOLOGICAL GESTURE

> *"So we may say that the* strength *of the movement stirs our will power in general; the* kind *of movement awakens in us a definite corresponding desire, and the* quality *of the same movement conjures up our feelings. Let us call them Psychological Gestures (hereinafter referred to as PG's), because their aim is to influence, stir, mold, and attune your whole inner life to its artistic aims and purposes".*
>
> Michael Chekhov, To the Actor, *Routledge Press, revised, 2002, courtesy of the Michael Chekhov Estate*

Lisa Dalton, Co-Founder and President of NMCA, has often said: "Psychological Gesture is the cherry on the top of the Chekhov cake".

The concept behind psychological gesture is that it can fuel an entire performance, once it is created and you have imbued it with all that you need to motivate and inspire you. Famous actors who have used this technique include Anthony Hopkins to Jack Nicholson, who mentioned his working with the psychological gesture on the Golden Globes Award show in 1999. Finding that overall gesture can be a tall order and even Michael Chekhov admitted that while for some performances this came rather easily, for others it did not come at all. If you aren't finding it to represent an entire performance, you can use the psychological gesture, or PG as it is often referred to, for scenes or even for specific moments. The PG is a way for you to create a physical manifestation of a character's journey, whether it's the arc for the entire story or a small portion of that story. If you are following this book's chapters, you have already practiced the archetypal gestures, working with the breath and full-body expression. Those gestures are simply done via your will force. For the PG, you now add the "why" and the "how" – a specific quality related to the character and role – to the "what" that you are already doing. In this way, you now incorporate that objective of the character, and begin to realize what it means if the character achieves this objective or "wins" or what happens if they "lose". One example is that you may be pushing as you did the with archetypal gesture, but you now have the objective of using the push aggressively to get rid of your competition. All of these choices now influence the gesture as you incorporate your thinking and feeling forces along with your willing force.

You will want to incorporate the Four Brothers of Art mentioned previously, being sure your gesture has a beginning, middle, and end for the sense of entirety, that the form is specific, that it encompasses artistic beauty and that you can perform it with a sense of ease. You will want to use your breath, inhaling to prepare and exhaling on the exertion. As in previous exercises you will want to sustain your ending moment to infuse it with the energy you have created, letting it sink into you.

Additional parameters for the PG are that you incorporate your full body and your full commitment to a gesture that, for you, conjures up the character's journey in any given story. Now – how do you achieve this lofty goal? There are three distinct ways as codified by NMCA and they are known as the "Three I's".

Improvisation 1: Inspiration/Imagination/Intellect

Improvisation requires having faith that some idea will come to you and to start this journey to discover your PG, you certainly need to have that faith. This is due to the fact that the first "I" of the discovery series is *inspiration*. It would be terrific if we all could consistently live in a state of inspiration, but typically finding inspiration requires concentration.

To proceed, pick a character which you are quite familiar with, which may be one you are currently working on or one that is well-known to you, which may range from Cinderella to Hamlet. Once chosen, start to focus on the journey of that character and imagine that you will know what the gesture is for that journey. Trust that it will simply come to you, and you will know how to move your body with one breath and full effort to represent that journey. The wonderful truth is that even if nothing comes to you, just pretend. Isn't acting pretending? Or simply move on to one of the other ways to explore PG. Once you've spent a bit of time lost in the story of your chosen character and being receptive to your inspiration to provide a full-body gesture, then begin those movements. Again, if inspiration didn't strike, just start to move with the idea of the character's journey in mind and something is sure to happen. If this first "I" is working for you, continue to refine the gesture so that you feel you could use this as preparation or as a reminder at any time within a story for you to connect with the character's journey. Work with your breath – inhaling to prepare and accepting the inspiration, exhaling on the action of the gesture and then sustaining the final position and finding the breath as needed that allows that sustaining. The sustaining of the gesture may be as brief as a few seconds or if you are experiencing the energy and desires of the character in that moment you may hold it and let it encompass you.

The second "I" is to access this gesture via your imagination and visualization. With a known character in mind, allow your character to improvise rather than you this time. See the character in your imagination, visualize the character, and then ask the character to show you the PG for their journey. Take a bit of time as your character (or your own imagination), may be reluctant at first but often if you remain concentrated on the visualization you will see your character present a gesture. Once you have seen that picture in your imagination, start to move with that gesture, refining as needed to allow the gesture to be energized and utilizing your whole body, and incorporating the Four Brothers, of ease, beauty, form, and wholeness. Let whatever your character gave you in your imagination become your inspiration, but feel free to now engage the entire body and breath to fully create your PG.

Perhaps you couldn't access a gesture from these first two "I's". As has been previously mentioned, there is no right or wrong to any of this work, simply different approaches, and you choose what works best for you. The third "I" is Intellect, and it allows you to craft a PG via your own thought processes and skill at analysis. Once you know your character and their journey through the story you have chosen, think about the sense of wholeness/entirety. Starting with the beginning, where is that for your character? Are they wildly successful and the journey is a succession of falls throughout the story? Are they downtrodden and the journey is uplifting and headed toward a glorious ending? You can now equate this beginning state with winning or losing. How can you create a gesture for this state? Is the character losing and being contracted into a small ball connects you with the psychological state that feels appropriate for this loss? Is your character winning and expanding with a wide-legged stance and arms outreached allowing you to feel the psychological state of the character? Now you have a starting point.

Next, think about how this character ends their journey – is it in a state of losing or winning? Is it a Cinderella type story where the character is happy ever after? If so, what would be your gesture to depict that state of happiness? Might it be arching backward with hands on the belly that is filled with laughter? Could it be that one foot is pointed forward and a hand is outstretched to show the world their new-found wealth? You can always think of the archetypal gestures in order to inspire these gestures. Again, these gestures have no limit, and your imagination is a powerful tool that can provide you with an endless variety of options which can be specific to each character you might play. Now that you have developed these win and loss gestures, it's time to fill in the "middle".

For the middle gesture, examine the "how" of the character's journey. How is it they build up to their win or how is it that they come to a point of loss in the story? This middle gesture may come to you organically or perhaps you require some practical assistance. Think about the ten archetypal gestures mentioned previously in Chapter 4. These are an excellent way to find a gesture for the how that can connect the win and loss. Does the character gather information in order to succeed? Do they pull others into their journey and it's that assistance that allows them to win? Were they lifting others which then allowed them to be lifted in turn? Did they push others away and that led to their downfall? Were they gathering but with greed which led to their demise? The combinations are endless when you incorporate pushing, pulling, smashing, lifting, gathering, throwing, reaching, dragging, penetrating, and tearing. While you have these at your fingertips via the Michael Chekhov technique, you may come up with your own word to describe the "how", which is of course, perfect! Perhaps you are winding your way in your journey, or you kick your way to success. The only criteria for you to remember is that you incorporate your full body with a maximum of energy and a complete breath so that the PG can compel you into the action required of your character.

Perhaps you chose Shakespeare's Macbeth as your character. An idea would be that Macbeth begins very optimistically – he will gain the throne so the beginning gesture may be both hands to the head as if feeling a crown with legs tightly together and the entire body reaching upwards to the sky with a gesture of dominance. You may decide that Macbeth's journey is that of greedily gathering to achieve his objective of being king – gathering information from the witches and gathering his wife's help to succeed. Gathering at a quick tempo, perhaps with a staccato rhythm, may awaken the greed that you ascribe to Macbeth. Then there is the ultimate failure at the end when Macbeth literally loses his head. The full-bodied gesture for this might be a journey to your knees, ending on the floor with the head tucked, signifying the ultimate loss.

On a lighter note, you may be working on the character of Cinderella. Cinderella's beginning gesture may be close to the ground, reminiscent of her stepmother forcing her to pick lentils out of the fireplace ashes. Her objective at this point may be to survive, and she is feeling loss. You might choose lifting as the "how" Cinderella changes her circumstances, as she intends to climb out of her lowly status. She also attempts to lift those around her, no matter how mean they may be. The ending for Cinderella may be a wide curtsy as she feels she has won her objective and enjoys sharing her appreciation with the royal entourage and her subjects, now that her status has been lifted.

The above are simply examples, and you have endless possibilities within you and with these tools that Michael Chekhov has provided to create your own unique PG. The PG is a moving creation, so while some of the descriptions may appear to be more static poses, it will be the entire journey of your gesture that can inspire your performance. Once you have your three elements you want to flow them together into one inspirational movement that requires your full concentration and can be easily repeated. While typically movement begins with an inhalation on preparation and an exhalation on the effort, and the PG should be achieved in one breath cycle, you might discover that inhaling and exhaling in a different order works best for you. Perhaps you begin with no air, as Cinderella might, feeling defeated by as she lifts and rises to curtsey, she fills with air, giving her a joyous buoyancy. Macbeth may begin full of air, using that air up while greedily grabbing and completely out of breath at the end of his sad journey. Again, these choices are for you to make, and you choose what inspires and motivates you the most. Allow yourself to experience the journey of the PG, not just a series of poses, as you combine them together into one expression that inspires the trajectory of your character.

Once you have the breath, you can flow from one gesture to the next, creating one full-body movement, or now one complete gesture that morphs from one form to another, and once you do, repeat it. Repetition allows the PG to settle within you and for you to be permeated by all that it gives you. You may now choose to do this PG prior to each rehearsal of a production and even backstage before heading out into the story. On a film set you may remind yourself where on the journey you are by repeating the portion of the gesture that relates to the section of the story you are working on, which is often not in sequence. You may discover that the PG works with your body and breath to influence your voice, which may organically alter depending on your PG and your body and breath changes. Allowing the voice to morph on its own in a healthy way will result in body and voice being connected via the characterization inspired by the PG.

The above work was improvisational in nature but did require that a known character was used. Now time to improvise using the technique of the PG with characters that you get to originate.

Improvisation 2: Time to mingle

Utilizing the characters and PG you just worked with, now mingle in the room as your character. Ideally this works if you are all choosing characters from the same script, but can also be more improvisational and increase your need to focus if characters are from a variety of times and places. You know what you want to win and can react accordingly, letting your winning gesture inform your actions. You know now what happens physically when you lose and can also incorporate that gesture based on your improvisational interactions with others. As you meet another character, see if they may be able to help you achieve your character's objective – to help you "win". Continue to interact throughout the group and identify the other characters that may assist you and those that may not. The leader may choose to call out "Freeze!" at any time and have everyone remain focused on their characters but take time to watch a duo or trio interact and observe how the gestures created via the PG now come alive when communicating. Then the group improvisation resumes, and the "Freeze!" can be used again until all participants have had a chance to be spotlighted.

Improvisation 3: The job interview

This improvisation will be at an employment agency. Someone is chosen to be the interviewer at the agency and plays center stage. Everyone is given a slip of paper with an assigned job that is their specialty and their winning gesture, their loss gesture, and one of the archetypal gestures to give them the "how" they work toward achieving their objective. It is also helpful to use other terms from the Michael Chekhov technique to provide them with the general form of their win or loss gesture, such as contracting, expanding, floating, or flying. The overall objective for each potential employee in the improv is to get a job, but the how will be very different. Imagine one employee gathering which may wind up embracing their employer while another tries to push their way into a job. As always, be sure to establish the consensual boundaries for any physical contact that may happen in the improv prior to starting. This consent may have already been established by the group but it's always helpful to quickly check in on each new day should boundaries alter.

Examples (you'll need to fill in the how/why for these basics, according to your character):

- Job: Landscaper Win: Expand Lose: Contract How: Reaching
- Job: Opera Singer Win: Float Lose: Fall How: Dragging

Everyone involved in the improv is given a bit of time to establish their PG, working to find a flow between their win and loss, and working with the "how" that they are given. Playing with tempo and rhythm can vastly alter the gesture and should be encouraged. The employer also has a win, loss, and how gesture which they can incorporate as part of the interview process. The preparation time should be relatively short as everyone ideally will have already improvised different ways of finding the PG while using a character. Now the character is new and based on their occupation, with the Michael Chekhov techniques incorporated to make finding the PG a briefer process. Always remind participants that there is now right or wrong, but this is an improvisation to express artistic creativity – go for it!

If you have a door, potential employees can wait behind the door, perhaps dividing the group in half so one half plays while the other is the audience, and then switch. In an open space the potential employees can circle around, coming up from the audience, and return to the audience once their interview has concluded. This way everyone stays present to see what occurs at the employment office. For this improvisation, performers should be encouraged to fully express their gestures during their interview, though some veiling will allow the interactions to be more realistic. You want to be sure you experience what the PG can do once established. The PG can provide the character with physicalized moments of wins and losses throughout the story and create a wonderful roller coaster ride of emotion for the audience to witness. For the purpose of the improvisation, you can go further physically than you might in a production, in order to more fully experience your wins and losses. If you have a time constraint the leader of the exercise may ring a bell or be sure the employer has an idea of how much time to spend with each applicant.

For an actual production, the PG may remain completely invisible, or facets of it may leak out at times, which will be choices made by the actor and director. Having the ability to rehearse and allowing all aspects of the PG to manifest fully physically, is a dynamic way to discover a variety of moments within the story. Discovering when the character feels they are winning and when they are losing and expressing those moments physically can add great dimension to a production. It's important for the actor to think about when their character is winning – as the audience may realize they aren't winning at all, and that contradiction can make it even more exciting to watch. Similarly, with losing – the character may be expressing loss, but the audience is rooting for them.

Improvisation 4: Time for school! (contributed by Lisa Loving Dalton, Professional Actor/Director/Educator, Co-Founder and President of NMCA)

This improvisation can be done early on as participants are becoming familiar with the psychological gesture, to make them more aware of the connection of the body and action to the psychology.

A group will divide in half, with each forming a long line and partners standing opposite each other, in the formation of a hallway. Participants on one side are given the character of "parent", while the participants on the other side are given the character of "young student". In everyone's imagination, there is an extremely busy and dangerous street between the parent and child. However, in this improvisation, the leader secretly informs those playing the children that they don't want to get on the bus which is on their side of the road and instead would rather cross the street and come back home. The parent must convince their child to get on the bus and not to cross the street. To make the improvisation even more urgent, the parents are told they are single parents and if they are late for work, they will lose their job, so they must convince their child to get on the bus immediately. The leader may also choose to run in between the two lines, representing the zooming traffic in between the parents and children.

The improvisation commences with the parents' objective being to get their child to board the bus, while the child's objective is to solicit permission from their parent to come back home.

Discussion/Reflection

What sort of gestures occurred as the parent and child interacted? Could you feel that your gestures were directly related to your psychology – what you were trying to achieve and what you were feeling? Was there one overarching gesture that represented your objective and could you use your full body to express it?

Wrap up

Explore psychological gestures via inspiration, imagination, and intellect. Improvise with a chosen character that you are familiar with, allowing that character to express wins and losses with others. Improvise as a potential employee interviewing for a job and experience how the PG influences behavior as you feel yourself winning or losing.

Solo application

When working on your own with a character, try the "Three I's" to determine what the PG for your character might be. See what your intuition and inspiration give you, and even if nothing seems to manifest you can pretend – just try something. Next, utilize your imagination to lead you to a gesture which may come from visualizing your character and how they move, and finally think about the way your character wins, loses, and how they go about getting what they want.

Script application

You may be able to analyze your character's entire journey in a production and create a PG that is fitting. Fully physically express the character's loss with a gesture, and their win with a gesture and what is the archetypal gesture representing the "how" as they pursue their objectives. You may then note these gestures throughout the script as to when you are winning and losing, which may result in some veiled use of the gestures – or simply provide underlying intent which may only come through the voice or the eyes. You may also use this process for individual scenes, as in any one scene you may experience both wins and losses and being able to have experienced the psychology of those wins/losses through gesture can allow you to better fill these moments. An example would be if your objective in a scene is to dismiss someone, your "how" might be to push them, tear them, smash them – depending on the gravity of the situation. If you are winning, that gesture might be expanding with joy for your achievement, while your loss might be contracting in defeat. The uniqueness will happen in how you represent that joy or defeat and of course you could contract with joy, doubled-over with laughter, or expand with defeat, reaching out all around you with frustration. Allow the character and your imagination to guide you.

Life application

If you would like to try, this is a great exercise to apply to one of your personal objectives in life. What is a physical gesture that allows you to feel a "win" if you were to accomplish a chosen goal? How do you physicalize feeling the loss if your goal is not achieved? What is the physical manifestation of the "how" – the way you will pursue this goal? Practicing this on a daily basis could be compared to an affirmation – but it's fully physicalized and therefore can propel you into action.

Index

acting: alternatives to using own personal experiences 85–86; appearing easy 22; on-camera 53, 64; diverse possibilities of Chekhov's techniques 36, 47; emotional recall, use of 86; incorporating improvisation lessons into future roles 16; individual work 106, 184; "Method" 60, 86; as pretending 22, 87, 121; shyness of some actors 121–122; in silence 65; on stage and in everyday life 47; transforming through movement 5; and veiling 53
Adler, Stella 86–87
Air, element of 36
alignment, physical 6–7, 49
angel walk exercise 66–70; "catching" the walker 67–68; consent for touching 67; holding hands 67, 68; light touching 67; outdoor setting version 69–70; taking turns 68; without touching or close contact 68–69; *see also* radiating and receiving techniques
anger, quality of 12, 16, 93
animal and creature work 43–44, 116–117
archetypal gestures 47–57; breath, noticing 48; changing the tempo 51–52; discussing/reflecting on 53, 55, 56; the drag 51; engaging the whole body 48; the gather 50; guiding principle 48; improvisational exercises 49–51, 54, 56; intention, with 52, 53–55; life application 57; the lift 50; making discoveries 51–52; meaning of "archetypal" 47; not carrying a positive or negative connotation 54; the penetration 51; primal 47; psychological forces improvisations 137; and psychological gesture 190, 193; the pull 49, 51, 55; the push 49, 51, 52, 55; quality, applying to the gesture 52; the reach 50; script application 57; sensations 52; the smash 49–50, 51, 52; solo application 57; speed dating 55–56; switching roles 55; the tear 51; the throw 50; veiling 47, 52–53, 55; wrap up 56–57
Arndt, Geoffrey 92–93
art: becoming the artist improvisation 142; every moment onstage as a work of 21; Four Brothers of Art *see* Four Brothers of Art techniques; improvisation as 41; movements as a work of 25, 32, 35; museums 141; psychological forces improvisations 142; *see also* artistic beauty; artistic center exercise
artistic beauty 22, 23, 26, 28, 29, 31, 32, 127, 188
artistic center exercise 98–99, 100, 101, 105
atmospheres 2, 145–158; atmosphere molecules 149–151; atmosphere

INDEX

orchestra 149; of beaches 145; birthday party exercise 151–152; cemetery at midnight scenario 146; champagne bubbles example 148; changes in 8, 10; choices based on 146; contraction and expansion exercises 8, 10, 11; discussing/reflecting on 147–148, 149, 151–152; of events 147; life application 158; limitless imagery 148; naming or baptizing of 148; overall atmospheres 146–148; personal 150–152, 158; post-writing 156; script application 157; solo application 157; Thanksgiving Stories, United States 152–156; wrap up 156

audiences: blocking out 173; "callers," as 80, 180; duos with 167–168; energy received from 174; input from 180–181; interacting with 173–174; moveable centers, techniques exploration exercises 103–104

auditions 23, 32, 61, 62, 94, 183

balancing sensation 75, 76, 78, 79, 81

beauty, cultivating sense of 21–25, 33; artistic beauty 22, 23, 26, 28, 29, 31, 32, 127, 188

BEEF (Beauty, Ease, Entirety and Form) game 24, 29–33

blindfolds, working with 25–28, 31, 67, 69, 89, 90–92

brain 10–11

breath, engaging with/noticing 31, 48, 70, 80, 99, 117, 165, 192; during balancing 76; changes in the breath 7, 8, 124–125, 165, 192; ease, breathing with 33, 99; holding the breath 76; sensations 74, 75, 76, 81; shallow or deep breathing 76; in stillness 162; tempo/rhythm exercises 163, 164, 165

Brothers of Art *see* Four Brothers of Art techniques

Browning, Joann 140

"callers" 80, 82, 170, 180; audience members as 128; instructors as 170

calmness 18, 33, 75, 94, 100, 169; in adversity 171; movement qualities 38, 45; radiating and receiving techniques 60, 62; stage fright, calming 173

characters, exploring: archetypal gestures 48; characters' names (not actors') used 42; Cinderella 157, 189–192; contraction and expansion exercises 5, 6, 8, 13–16; creating through costume 123; dropping/returning to ("home base") concept 86, 97–98; emotional recall, use of 86; finding one's own version 102; greetings *see* greetings; Macbeth 191, 192; moveable centers concept 97–98, 102, 104–106, 117; movement qualities 35–36, 38, 39; nature, characters from 112–113, 119; open-ended statements (e.g. "My name is") 102, 118, 125, 126, 129; predominantly a thinking, feeling or will-force character, whether 133, 134, 138, 139, 142; primary essence 157; psychological gesture, with 188–194; radiating or receiving 59–60, 71; remaining in character 16, 56, 103; sensational characters 90–91; "sour" or "sweet" characters 91, 92; tempo and rhythm, with 171; visualizing 110–112, 115, 178, 189; voice 102, 154, 155, 156; *see also* acting; contraction and expansion techniques; costume exercises; imaginary body techniques; imagining; moveable centers concept

Chekhov, Michael: *To the Actor* 5, 21, 35, 59, 85, 97, 121, 133, 187; actor at Moscow Art Theatre 86; on atmospheres 145, 152–153; characterization tools 153; on contraction and expansion 14; on creative imagination 74; on jewelry in technique 104, 105; physicality of Chekhov's technique 5; on power of imagination 109–110; on rhythm 164; Square Dance Calls 170; student of Stanislavski 86; on the subconscious 116; teaching at Dartington Hall, England (1930s) 37; on transformation 121; on veiling 47, 52–53; *see also* Chekhov Square Dance; Michael Chekhov estate; NMCA (National Michael Chekhov Association)

Chekhov Square Dance 169–170

Chenard, Josh 169–170

choreography 48

Cinderella character 157, 189–192

circles, working in 13, 39, 40, 64, 86, 90, 98, 99, 155, 169, 170; circles of

INDEX

concentration 173; concentric circles 77; costume characters improvisations 122, 123, 125; inner circles 77–78, 149–150; mirror circles 82; outer circles 78, 149, 150; semi-circles 49, 69
clay analogy, molding 37
close-ups 53, 55, 64–65
Colvin, Jack 73
communication 22, 45, 56–57, 60, 83, 89, 149, 183, 193; empathy 83; sensations, influencing 79; using only the eyes 64, 65; via veiling 52–53
compassion 71
contraction and expansion techniques 5–18; atmosphere, changes in 8, 10, 11; awareness of states 18; body language, awareness of 10; breath, noticing 7, 8; characters, exploring 5, 6, 8, 13–16; closed-off, contracted heart 8–9; comical secret, contracting with 11, 12, 16; contracted mind 10, 16; discussing/reflecting on 7–8, 12–15, 16; emotions, creating through 6, 8, 13; expanded mind 11, 16; expand-ers/contract-ers convention *see* expand-ers/contract-ers convention; expanding while angry 12; feeling closed off 17–18; good/bad interpretations of contracted/expanded states 8; letting go/coming back to neutral 9–13; life application 17–18; neither having only positive or negative connotations 15; numerical noting of expanded/contracted states 17; open, expanded heart 9; physical movement 6–8, 9, 10–11, 16; playing with applicable qualities 16–17; psycho-physical 5–6, 74, 90, 164, 166; script application 17; shaking out 10, 11, 12; solo application 17; switching roles 16; teamwork 14–16
costume exercises 121–131; character creation 123; creative costumes 122–123; developing 123; discussing/reflecting on 123, 124, 127; improvisation example 130; interaction, costumer character 124–125; interviews 128–131; life application 131; presenting solo as a trio 127–128; script application 131; solo application 122, 131; variations 129, 130; walk the runway exercise 123–124; working as a model or fashion stylist 123–124; wrap up 130
costume relay race improvisation 27–29, 31
curiosity 87, 88
Cutting, Blair 60, 109

Dalton, Lisa 1, 29–33, 60, 73, 173, 187
dancing puppets exercise 25–27, 31
deep breathing 116, 154; *see also* breath, engaging with/noticing
dialogue 41, 70, 80, 92, 118, 127, 171; and moveable center techniques 102, 103
duos, working in 13, 26, 103, 180; audiences, with 168–169; costume exercises 126; qualities of movement exercises 39, 42, 44; radiating and receiving techniques 65; rhythm, playing with 168–169; sensations, exploring 78, 79–80

Earth 36
ease, sense of 99, 101, 178; breathing with 33, 99; costume characters improvisations 124, 127; Four Brothers of Art techniques 21–33; moving with 22, 26, 170; psychological gesture 188, 189; *see also* Four Brothers of Art techniques
emotions: creating through contraction/expansion techniques 6, 8, 13; emotional recall 86; general persona 150; letting go of 86; qualities of 93; strong 88; *see also* anger, quality of; fear, quality of; psychological forces improvisations; Three Sister sensations, exploring
empathy 18, 57, 83
energy 7, 13, 23, 41, 45; of anger 12; audiences, received from 174; boundless 35, 63; dragging 51, 106; eye contact, sending through 54, 55; fiery 37–38; gathering 49; imaginary ball of 50, 99, 100, 106; internal 52; kinesphere (bubble of energy) 61–63; line of 99; optimistic 62; pulling 49; radiating 61, 64, 69, 70, 71; receiving 9, 62–63, 66, 67; sending 38, 49, 51, 53, 54, 60–62, 65, 66; states of 64; upward flow of 50; and veiling 52; *see also* radiating and receiving techniques

equilibrium, states of 73
expand-ers/contract-ers convention 14–18; break rooms 15, 16; qualities of expansion or contraction, portraying 15; set up 14–15
eye contact 53, 54, 77, 176; direct 174, 175, 179, 183; establishing 78; maintaining 177

falling sensation 74, 76, 77, 79, 81
fear, quality of 88
feeling 135–136, 141; *see also* emotions; psychological forces improvisations; psychological gesture (PG)
flexibility, in performance 48
floating sensation 74–81; downward movement 75; upward movement 73
flowing 36–39, 41–44; going with the flow 38; *see also* movement qualities, exercises involving
flying 35–40, 42; *see also* movement qualities, exercises involving
focal points 173–184; audience input 180–181; ball catch with 176–178; ball toss chaos 178; circles of concentration 173; enriching the passing moments of a role 181–183; feeling out in space 176, 177–178; five, discovering 174–176; group work 176–180; immediate situation 182; inner monologue of 178–180; life application 184; looking at oneself 174; observing the environment 175, 177; outside the immediate situation 182; personal experience 181–182; script application 183–184; situation 182–183; solo application 183; theatrical monologues 175; thinking of something specific 175, 177; working with others 174–175, 178; working with peer participants 176–177; working with self 174, 176, 177, 178; wrap up 183
form 28, 32, 33, 35, 188, 192; bodily 23, 25, 112; costume relay race improvisation 27, 28, 31; dancing puppets exercise 25, 26, 27, 31; Four Brothers of Art techniques 21–25, 27–29, 31–33, 127, 189; free-form improvisation 23, 39, 48, 56
Four Brothers of Art techniques 21–33; BEEF (Beauty, Ease, Entirety and Form) game 24, 29–33; benefits of 22; chairs, working with 22–24; costume relay race improvisation 27–29, 31; dancing puppets exercise 25–27, 31; discussing/reflecting on 25, 27, 28; every moment onstage as a work of art 21; imagining and following a plan 29; incorporating into costume exercises 127; incorporating into one's own being 24–25; incorporating into psychological gesture 189; life application 32–33; moving without props 25; script application 32; solo application of 32; switching roles 26; taking turns 28; traits, outline of 21–22; visceral experience of 27; wrap up 31–32; *see also* beauty, cultivating sense of; ease, sense of; flowing; form
Four Elements 36
FPs *see* focal points
free-form improvisation 23, 39, 48, 56; free-form imaginary body 110–112
freezing 42, 61, 125, 167, 193; artistic center exercise 98–99; freeze and drop 77–78; freeze and share 102–103; and unfreezing 79, 103, 118, 138, 168

gestures: freezing 98–99; and greetings 117; joint-on-joint 135, 137, 138; natural and usual 47; thumbs, use of 136, 139; *see also* archetypal gestures; psychological gesture (PG)
greetings 40, 78, 82, 91; contraction and expansion techniques 9–11, 13; imaginary body techniques 117; moveable center, exploration exercises 101, 102; veiled 76–77; *see also* voice
group work: atmospheres 149–151; character centers 102; contraction and expansion 6; focal points 176–180; Four Brothers of Art 23; moveable centers 102–103; movement qualities 43–44; psychological gesture 193; radiating and receiving techniques 63–64; *see also* teamwork, exercises incorporating

Hamilton, Nichole 80–83
heart: angry 12; closed-off, contracted 8–9, 10, 16; open, expanded 9, 10, 16

Hurley, Paul 43–44, 140–142
Hutchinson, Anjalee Deshpande 152–156

iambic pentameter 171
ideal artistic enter *see* artistic center exercise
imaginary body technique 109–119; animals 116–117; "ani-morphosis" 118; breath work 117; characters from nature 112–113, 119; concept of imaginary body 109; discussing/reflecting on 112, 113–114, 116, 117; free-form 110–112; greetings 118; interactions 117–118; life application 119; museum exercise 113, 114; portraits/photographs/cartoons, use of 114–116; script application 119; self-transformation 110; solo application 119; wrap up 119; *see also* acting; characters, exploring; imagining
imagining: of clay 36, 37, 44; of fire 37–38; limitless imagination 109; moveable centers concept 98; and music 167–168; power of imagination 109; of rock 36, 44; and then following a plan 29; of water 37; *see also* imaginary body technique; moveable centers concept; visualization
India 153
individual work *see* solo application of improvisation techniques
inspiration 188–192
International Michael Chekhov Symposium (2007) 73
interviews, costume characters 128–131; *see also* costume exercises; job interview
invention convention exercise 40–42

Jackson, Tommy, Square Dance without Calls 170
job interview 32–33, 79, 106, 129, 130; psychological gesture improvisation 193–195; *see also* auditions; interviews, costume characters
joy, quality of 39, 88, 147; *see also* laughter

Kelly, Baron 181–183
kinesphere (bubble of energy) 61–63

Laban, Rudolph 37
laughter 12, 13, 104, 179, 190, 196; *see also* joy, quality of

legato rhythm 164, 171
life, application of improvisation techniques to: alternatives to using own personal experiences 85–86; archetypal gestures 57; atmospheres 158; balance 75; contraction and expansion 17–18; focal points 184; Four Brothers of Art 32–33; imaginary body 119; moveable centers 106; movement qualities 45; psychological forces 143; psychological gesture 196; qualities 94; radiating and receiving 71; rhythm and tempo 171; sensations 83, 94
Light 36
lines, rehearsing 13, 32, 82, 163
lines, working in 30, 70; radiating and receiving techniques 64, 67; techniques exploration exercises archetypal gestures 52, 55; techniques exploration exercises costume characters 126
Lobdell, Peter 60

Macbeth character 191, 192
Maturo, C. 128–131
"Method" acting 60, 86
Michael Chekhov Studio, New York City 2, 60, 109
mind, contraction and expansion 10–11, 12, 16
molding 35–39, 41–44; *see also* movement qualities, exercises involving
moment, being in 29, 86, 128, 168, 178; enriching the passing moments of a role 181–183
monologue: inner monologue, focal points 178–180; in object plays 81
moveable centers concept 97–106; altering the center 100–101; artistic center 98–99, 100, 101, 105; audiences, use of 103–104; changing the center 100; character work 97–98, 102, 104–106, 117; creating a "home base" 97–98; dialogue 102; discussing/reflecting on 99, 100, 101, 103, 104–105; freezing 102–103; greetings 101, 102; imagination, use of 98; interactions 101; jelly-like quality/jiggling center 100–101; life application 106; script application 106; solo application 106; suggested character centers 102; text with improvised centers 104–105; trio

of centers 105; upper chest, focus on 99, 101; walking through space exercise 99–101; wrap up 105–106
movement qualities, exercises involving 35–45; animal and creature work 43–44; architects' design of celebrity's home scenario 42; discussing/reflecting on 38–39, 40, 41, 43; everyday chat 39–40; fitness studio scenario 42; hello and goodbye greetings 40; invention convention 40–42; life application 45; pursuing objectives 42–43; radiating fire 38, 41, 43, 44; relating to the Four Elements 36; script application 45; solo application of 36, 45; switching roles 41; wrap up 44; *see also* flowing; flying; molding; radiating and receiving techniques
movements, copying in mirror exercise 77
muscle relaxation 115–116
music, rhythm in 166–167

National Michael Chekhov Association *see* NMCA (National Michael Chekhov Association)
National Shakespeare Conservatory, New York 60
nature imagery 70; characters from nature 112–113
neutral stance *see* universal stance
NMCA (National Michael Chekhov Association) 1, 2, 6, 47, 48, 161, 174
notebooks 153

objects, working with 49, 134, 181; balancing, falling and floating sensations 73, 80; floating objects 80; Four Brothers of Art techniques 24, 28, 30–32; gravitational pull 80–81; imaginary body techniques 112, 113, 117; object plays 80–83; open palm, handling with 135; picking up 6, 25, 81, 92, 112, 117, 128; qualities and sensations, techniques incorporating 87, 89–92; *see also* props
on-camera acting 64
opposites 14, 15, 16, 54

pandemonium, moving with 166, 169
pauses 23, 123, 173; cosmic 176; poignant 32, 178

personal atmosphere 150–151, 158; birthday party exercise 151–152
personal experience: alternatives to using 6, 85; focal points 181–182; personal state of expansion or contraction 17–18; *see also* life, application of improvisation techniques to
PG *see* psychological gesture (PG)
physicality, of Chekhov's technique 5
plan, following 28–29
Powers, Mala 1, 59, 71, 87, 110, 133, 148
props 127, 151, 168; focal points 176, 177, 178; and Four Brothers techniques 25, 28; movement qualities exercises 36, 40, 41; moving without 25; *see also* objects, working with
psychic connection 65
psychological forces improvisations 133–143; contracted or expanded mind *see* contraction and expansion techniques; creating art 142; discussing/reflecting on 137, 138, 140; experimenting with thinking, feeling or willing 141–142; feeling 133, 135–136; imbalance of thinking, feeling or willing 133; life application 143; moving through space 134–135; museum setting 140–142; new hospital scenario 137–138; party planning scenario 138–139; political debate scenario 140; predominantly a thinking, feeling or will-force character, whether 133, 134, 138, 139, 142; problem solving scenario 139–140; replays 137; script application 142–143; solo application 142; sounds associated with thinking, feeling or willing 135; thinking 133, 134–135; voice 135; will force 133, 136; Wizard of Oz archetypes exercise 136–137; wrap up 142
psychological gesture (PG) 187–197; and archetypal gestures 190, 193; characters, exploring 188–194; discussing/reflecting on 195; finding 187; Four Brothers of Art techniques, incorporating 189; full-body 189; inspiration 188–192; job interview scenario 193–195; life application 196; mingling in the room as a character 192–193; as a moving creation 191–192; parameters 188; parent and

child scenario 195; in a real production 194–195; script application 196; solo application 196; winning and losing 194–195, 196; wrap up 196
psycho-physical techniques 5–6, 74, 90, 164, 166
pursuing objectives exercise 42–43

qualities and sensations, techniques incorporating 85–94; anger 93; calmness 94; choosing to keep item in imaginary shop 92; curiosity 87, 88; discussing/reflecting on 88–89, 90, 99; duos, working in 91–92; everyday tasks 92–93; experiencing a variety of qualities 87–89; fear 88; journey through sensations 89–90; life application 94; sadness 93, 94; script application 93–94; sensational characters 90–91; shaking out 87, 88; solo application 87, 93; stimulating the senses through objects 89; trios, working in 91–92; wrap up 93; *see also* emotions; Three Sister sensations, exploring
qualities of movement exercises *see* movement qualities, exercises involving

radiating and receiving techniques 59–71; angel walk 66–70; characters, exploration exercises 59–60, 71; discussing/reflecting on 64, 65, 66; images/feelings to radiate 65, 66; kinesphere (bubble of energy) 61–63; life application 71; movement qualities 35; nature imagery 70; psychic connection 65; with qualities attached 65–66; radiating and sending energy (physical exercise) 60–62; radiating fire 35, 37–38, 42; receiving the energy (physical exercise) 62–63; scenarios 66, 70; script application 71; solo application 71; strolling through the park exercise 63–64; word, radiating 64–65; working back-to-back 65; wrap up 70; *see also* movement qualities, exercises involving
rehearsal 2, 12, 104; and costume characters 127, 131; and Four Brothers of Art techniques 29, 32; psychological gesture improvisation 192, 194

rhythms: combining with tempo 169; discussing/reflecting on 168; exploring 170; legato 164, 171; in music 166–167; pandemonium 166, 169; staccato 164–165; stillness 166, 168; walking through space exercise 100; waltz 165–166; working as if in a performance 167–168; *see also* tempo exercises
Rodin, François Auguste René, sculpture of 135, 138

sadness, quality of 93, 94
Schmidt, Suzanne 105
Schuld, Susan 70
scripts, application of improvisation techniques to: archetypal gestures 57; atmospheres 157; contraction and expansion 17; focal points 183–184; Four Brothers of Art 32; imaginary body 119; moveable centers 106; movement qualities 45; overall atmosphere of a script 157; psychological functions, techniques incorporating 142–143; psychological gesture 196; qualities and sensations 93–94; radiating and receiving 71; reviewing a script 17, 45; rhythm and tempo 171; sensations 83
Shakespeare, William 171, 191
shaking out 10, 11, 12
Shurtleff, Michael, *Audition* 14
side-coaching 15, 22, 77, 99, 103; archetypal gestures, exploration exercises 52, 54; audience input 180; movement qualities exercises 40–41; parent and child interaction 195
solo application of improvisation techniques: archetypal gestures 57; atmospheres 157; contraction and expansion techniques 6, 17; costume characters 131; focal points 183, 184; Four Brothers of Art 32; "home play" 17; imaginary body 119; moveable centers 106; movement qualities 36, 45; psychological forces 142; psychological gesture 196; qualities and sensations 87, 93; radiating and receiving 71; rhythm and tempo 171; script application 131; sensations 82–83
speed dating exercise 55–56

staccato rhythm 164–165
Stanislavski, Constantin 86–87, 161
stillness 162, 166, 168
Strasberg, Lee 86–87
subconscious 116

teamwork, exercises incorporating 78, 103; archetypal gestures 52, 54; atmospheres 149, 151; contraction and expansion 14–16; costume improvisations 123–126; Four Brothers of Art 24, 26, 27–29, 31; movement qualities 39, 42; qualities and sensations 89, 90; radiating and receiving 65, 66; rhythm 167, 168; thinking, feeling and willing 136, 137, 138, 139; Three Sisters sensations 78–79; *see also* group work
tempo exercises 36, 161–164, 168; and archetypal gestures 51–52; combining with rhythm 169; exploring 170; scales 162
tense/release exercises 115–116
Thanksgiving Stories, United States 152–156; collaborative writing 154–156; family lists 154; post-writing atmospheres 156; reading lists 153–154; Thanksgiving foods, listing 153; *see also* atmospheres
thinking: contraction and expansion techniques 10–11, 16; focal points 175, 177; psychological forces improvisations 134–135, 141; *see also* contraction and expansion techniques; psychological forces improvisations; psychological gesture (PG)
Three Sister sensations, exploring: archetypal gestures 52; balancing, falling and floating 73–83; chatting about the weather exercise 78–79; contraction and expansion techniques 8, 9, 12; discussing/reflecting on 76, 78, 79; life application 83; mirror exercise 77–78; monologue, in object plays 81; movement qualities 36; object plays 80–83; and qualities 85–94; within a scene 82; script application 83; solo application 82–83; switching roles 77; wrap up 82; *see also* falling sensation; floating sensation
threes, working in *see* trios, working in
touching 26–28, 65, 67, 86; actual touch 89; forbidden in COVID pandemic 68; of objects 30, 31; of other actors 30, 67, 89; touch of sound 100, 117, 125–126, 164–166
trios, working in 39–40, 139; *see also* dancing puppets exercise
twos, working in *see* duos, working in

unhelpful training techniques 2
universal stance 36, 49, 60, 87, 98; balanced 60, 61; contraction and expansion techniques 6–7, 8, 11; defining "universal" 60; describing 6–7

veiling 47, 52–53, 55, 106, 116, 134; defining 52; veiled greetings 76–77
visualization 110–112, 115, 178, 189; *see also* imagining
vocalizing 76, 102, 135; contraction and expansion techniques 7, 14; tempo and rhythm 163, 164, 166; as a thinking, feeling or willing character 143; *see also* voice
voice 180, 192, 196; altering the center 100–101; challenging 76; changes in 7–8, 165; of character 102, 154, 155, 156; connection to movement 164; imaginary body, exploring 117; low/whispering 179; new 101, 125; speaking 163; tempo/rhythm 30, 163–166, 168; thinking, representing 135; typical 100; *see also* greetings; tempo exercises; vocalizing

walking, when improvising: contraction and expansion techniques 9, 10–11; tempo scales 162–163; walking the runway exercise 123–124; walking through space exercise 99–101; *see also* angel walk exercise
Walters, Stephanie Kyung Sun 152
waltz rhythm 165–166
Water, element of 36; imagining water 37, 44, 70
wholeness/entirety, focus on 21–24, 26, 28, 29, 48
willing/will force 133, 136, 141, 142; *see also* psychological forces improvisations; psychological gesture (PG)
Wizard of Oz archetypes 136–137

For Product Safety Concerns and Information please contact our EU
representative GPSR@taylorandfrancis.com
Taylor & Francis Verlag GmbH, Kaufingerstraße 24, 80331 München, Germany